TALES OF THE
OLD GYPSIES

Members of the Church Army with hop-pickers in 1913

A Gypsy Encampment *by Sir Alfred Munnings, 1920*

TALES OF THE
OLD GYPSIES

JENNIFER DAVIES

DAVID & CHARLES

An old family photo from the collection of Jean Hudson (see The Harrisons of Skipton)

page 3 Gypsies at London Airport (detail) by Denis E. Harvey

A DAVID & CHARLES BOOK

First published in the UK in 1999
Copyright © Jennifer Davies 1999

Jennifer Davies has asserted her right to be identified as author of this work in accordance
with the Copyright, Designs and Patents Act, 1988.

A catalogue record for this book is available from the British Library.

ISBN 0 7153 0702 9

Printed in the UK by Butler & Tanner Limited
for David & Charles
Brunel House   Newton Abbot   Devon

CONTENTS

In memory of Stanley

O Beng te lel o bales te covel Kova lili!

Two bow-topped waggons belonging to Fred Price photographed near Pembroke, South Wales in August 1956 (Photo: G.E.C. Webb)

The Gipsy's Camp

How oft on Sundays, when I'd time to tramp,
My rambles led me to a gipsy's camp,
Where the real effigy of midnight hags,
With tawny smoked flesh and tattered rags,
Uncouth-brimmed hat, and weather-beaten cloak,
'Neath the wild shelter of a knotty oak,
Along the greensward uniformly pricks
Her pliant bending hazel's arching sticks:
While round-topt brush, or briar-entangled hedge,
Where flag-leaves spring beneath, or ramping sedge,
Keeps off the bothering bustle of the wind,
And give the best retreat she hopes to find.
How oft I've bent me o'er her fire and smoke,
To hear her givverish tale so quaintly spoke,
While the old Sybil forged her boding clack,
Two imps the meanwhile bawling at her back;
Oft on my hand her magic coin's been struck,
And hoping chink, she talked of morts of luck:
And still, as boyish hopes did first agree,
Mingled with fears to drop the fortune's fee,
I never failed to gain the honours sought,
And Square and Lord were purchased with a groat.
But as man's unbelieving taste came round,
She furious stampt her shoeless foot aground,
Wiped bye her soot-black hair with clenching fist,
While through her yellow teeth the spittle hist,
Swearing by all her lucky powers of fate,
Which like as footboys on her actions wait,
That fortune's scale should to my sorrow turn,
And I one day the rash neglect should mourn;
That good to bad should change, and I should be
Lost to this world and all eternity;
That poor as Job I should remain unblest:
(Alas, for fourpence how my die is cast!)
Of not a hoarded farthing be possesst,
And when all's done, be shoved to hell at last.

JOHN CLARE

George, Berti, Rodi (née Wainwright) and Jim Heron with a cottage-shaped or ledged waggon (Photo: Fred Shaw)

REAL GYPSIES NEVER WEAR EARRINGS...

'Real gypsies never wear earrings or have tattoos.' That's what a present-day gypsy sherro rom (head man) told me. I'm afraid one of my tale tellers does have tattoos but his parents were gypsies, also he paints gypsy waggons and travels and lives in one. Other contributors, the Coulson family, coal merchants and rag 'n bone men, have merely married into gypsy blood, but I've included them too, for they are fascinating in themselves. All this being so, if you are a purist (rather like the gypsiologists of the early part of this century), and only interested in the 'true' Romani, you may 'tut-tut'.

However, having said that, gypsies have been in Britain since the beginning of the 15th century and – human nature being what it is – it would be very surprising to find a family whose pedigree hasn't become diluted every now and again by gorgio (non-gypsy) blood. Take for example, 83-year-old Gevoner Locke. Gevoner's father, Charlie Locke, came from one of the oldest gypsy families in Wales but her mother was a gorgio who fell in love with the tall, handsome Charlie after seeing him play in a dance band!

Pedigrees aside, the story tellers in this book are a kind of their own. Their observations and values are gypsy and their stories and background threaded through with gypsy traits. For example gypsies adore their children, respect their elders, adhere to traditions, can be exciteable and superstitious, love 'showy' objects, respect fighters, enjoy anything to do with horses, caged birds or lurchers and, above all these, have an extraordinary ability to make something from very little.

Practically all the story tellers were self-employed, the women combining their work of hawking, rag collecting and field work with cooking and bringing up their families. The overall picture of their lives is that they were no idyll. A background so hard creates close-knit communities and a fighting spirit. Violet Smith, who has a chapter, once called out to a curious on-looker 'I'm proud to be a gypsy!'

Several contributors, because their families were constantly on the move, never had sufficient schooling to teach them to read and write. If this book does nothing else, it has given them an opportunity to record their stories for the next generation.

Archive material of varying lengths has been included. Some of it ties in with the story tellers' tales. Other bits are included because, I hope, they'll prove of interest.

THE HISTORY OF GYPSIES

The name 'gypsies' comes from 'Egyptians', because people believed that gypsies came from Egypt. However, in the late eighteenth and early nineteenth centuries scholars studying the gypsy's language of Romani found in it similarities to existing Indian dialects, and over the years, India has become accepted as their country of origin. It is generally believed today that they left India about 1,000 years ago, possibly ousted during religious wars. The exiles wandered gradually across the Middle East, possibly staying for some time in Egypt, reaching Europe around the fourteenth century.

The earliest record of them in Britain is in the accounts of 1505 of the Lord High Treasurer in Scotland, where they are referred to as 'Egyptians'. In 1514 a witness at an inquest in England referred to an Egyptian woman who had lodged in Lambeth and who could tell marvellous things by looking into one's hand.

The gypsies were at first made welcome, as people were fascinated by their fortune-telling, their skills as musicians and entertainers, and by their exotic colourfulness. However, those in authority began to fear that their itinerant ways would encourage people to vagrancy. There was also dissatisfaction in so far as the gypsies were difficult to tax, being unaccountable to any set area. An additional worry was that their trades – for example metalwork – took custom from local craftsmen. Finally, their dark looks and their 'foreign' demeanour were disliked and distrusted.

In 1530 a law was passed stipulating that they must leave Britain: those that did not would be imprisoned and their goods forfeited. This was replaced in 1554 by even harsher legislation, namely the death penalty for those who continued to pursue their nomadic ways; it also applied to anyone having contact with gypsies. Court records provide ample evidence of the persecution of gypsies in the ensuing years; for example, an entry in Gloucester Court Records for the Michaelmas Session of 1681 states that Francis Hand (Justice of the Peace) was to: 'consider what allowance to give John Townsend of the said Parish of Bitton for the charge he hath been at for supressing the Egiptians'. Penal sanctions against gypsies were not repealed until 1791.

Opposite: Old Sophie. George Dudfield, who was born in 1909, remembers her thus:
'Sophie's headquarters might have been Woolhope in Herefordshire. Her husband was named Donald and he wore a flat, black, clerical hat. They came through the Gloucestershire village of Dymock periodically and Sophie used to call in at my mother's house and ask her to write letters. There was a theory that Sophie came through Dymock to get tanked up with cider at Portway Top where Mr Harry Nunn had a small farm on which he made cider.'

Overleaf: Members of the Church Army with hop-pickers in 1913

Charlie and Andrew Price with their waggons on Appleby Hill in 1956. These kinds of waggons can still occasionally be seen on the approach roads to big horse fairs (Photo: T.A. Clarke)

Despite the hardships of gypsy life, and the prejudices against it, such an existence nevertheless proved fascinating to non-gypsies. One of the most celebrated tales of a gorgio turned gypsy is that of Bampfylde Moore Carew (1693–1770?). His family once inhabited Carew Castle in Pembrokeshire, but by Carew's time most of them were living in the West Country. Carew's father was the Rector of Bickleigh, near Tiverton, and Carew attended Blundell's School in Tiverton. One day whilst playing truant from the school, Carew and another schoolboy came across a band of gypsies enjoying a feast. They joined in, and Carew was so taken with the gypsies that he became one of their band. He learned every trick that they could teach him, and became quite accomplished at begging for money, using as his props various convincing disguises and hard luck stories.

Carew was a wanderer, and leaving the gypsies he took passage on a ship to Newfoundland. On his return he disembarked at Dartmouth with a Newfoundland dog; this breed is big enough to pull a child in a cart, and so proved a suitably impressive companion for Carew's forthcoming role. He rejoined the gypsies; Clause Patch their leader died, and Carew was elected 'King of the Gypsies' in his place.

All the better informed after the experience of his sea voyage, Carew posed as a distressed seaman and conned money from various noblemen. He was arrested and deported to America, but escaped when the ship landed there; he posed as a Quaker, and managed to make his way back to England. Some time later he was sent on a convict ship a second time – but again escaped as soon as the ship docked, eventually returning to Bristol. His wife then persuaded him to go back to his aristocratic family, who accepted him on the condition that he'd give up his gypsy life. Carew agreed, and gave up begging and resigned his gypsy kingship; nevertheless he assured the gypsies of his lasting affection for them.

And the real gypsies who had no such easy refuge to fall back on, what of them? In the nineteenth century they enjoyed a period of relative quiet, and were left to travel and trade in peace. By the middle of the twentieth century, however, many of their traditional money-earners were becoming old-fashioned – trades such as horse-dealing, peg- and flower-selling, making and repairing household metalware, and seasonal farmwork, were simply not wanted. Also the growing popularity of motor vehicles meant that it was increasingly difficult for them to find craftsmen to maintain their horse-drawn waggons.

In the 1950s many gypsies ceased travelling and bought land on which to settle. However, the Caravan Sites and Control of Development Act 1960 stopped this practice, because site owners had to comply with such stringent regulations in order to obtain a licence. The act was really aimed at preventing an uncontrolled rash of holiday caravan sites. By this time gypsy work had become more dependent on motor transport, largely in the form of lorries; it included scrap dealing; tree lopping; tarmacing; barn painting; selling farm gates and so on – all occupations which were self-employed and mobile.

In 1968, counties were ordered to provide sites for gypsies, although often the gypsy population was not catered for, and government reorganisation in 1974 didn't help the situation, either.

In 1986, fears of 'hippy' invasions led to a Public Order Act; this strengthened police powers to evict not only hippy settlements, but gypsies too. Then in 1994 the Criminal Justice Act repealed the ruling that county councils should provide gypsy sites, but it also gave the police and the local authorities the power to move gypsies on. That year it was calculated that there were 4,000 gypsy families with no legal stopping place, and this is an issue which continues to anger and concern gypsies.

Gypsy communities remain close-knit, and they hold on to their traditions. Today, even as years ago, their existence creates a mixed reaction of tolerance and prejudice.

Gypsy superstitions

To see someone with a cloven (clubbed) foot is very unlucky.

To see a cross-eyed person is unlucky.

Never look behind if you're following a coffin in a funeral procession because if you do you'll see another one soon.

It's unlucky to turn back if you've forgotten something.

PÄKKED PÄSH O KRÄLLISSAS GAV. (TOLD NEAR WINDSOR)

Janet Tuckey (Published 1874)

It is not known whether this commemorates a true event. However, Queen Victoria does make particular note in her girlhood diaries of the bleak winter's day when her mother sent food and clothes to a young gypsy woman, her newborn baby and the rest of the family. The seventeen-year-old Princess wrote how unhappy and grieved she had been that the gypsies should perish and shiver for want but now they had been helped she could go to bed happy.

'LOOK, brother—tell me if you know
      'DORDI, mi pal—ko jívela
Who lives in that big castle there?'
      Adré boro ker adoi?'
'The Queen, you stupid! Now don't go
      'Tu dínnelo chal, I krállissa!—
A-sayin' you've ne'er heard of *her*.
      Mä pen tu's kékker shüned o' yoi!

'For she's a right good lady—yes,
      'Yeck küshti räni—ävali:
She loves the poor, ay, that she do'
      Yoi kämela o chóro müsh.
And she can feel for the distress
      Te yói's sä síg 'dré läkis see
Of wandering folk like me and you.
      For sär I käli fókis düsh.

'*And how do I know that?* Well, hark:
      'Sä mandy sosti jin o' lis?
One day last year my wife and me
      Del kan: adre o waver besh
Were travelling by Windsor Park—
      Mandy te miri romani
Those trees out yonder, do you see?
      Sos pirryin' pash o krallis wesh.

'My wife and me were going along
          'Mandy te miri romani
Towards Windsor—just afore you there—
          Sos jallin keti gav acai;
The children, all together, clung
          Te moro chavos, ketterni,
Upon the back of our old mare.
          Beshed pre o dumo o'ye gry.

'But my poor girl said: "Stop a bit
          "Oh, hatch a koosi, deari rom,"
And let me rest, oh husband dear!
          Mi poori juva penela;
I can't go further, I'm not fit;
          "Ma jal anduro – kinlo shom! –
Just set our little tent up here."
          Kair moro bitti tan kenna."

'That was a wintry day, my lad!
          'Sos yeck wenesto divvus, pal:
One whiteness over all the place;
          O puv sos pano sarapre;
The bitter north-wind blew like mad;
          O bavol pudered fon shimal;
The snow came stinging in one's face.
          O yiv pelled surrelo tuley.

'I tell you 'twas no easy task
          'Sos dush ta hatch a tan adoi
In all that cold to pitch a tent;
          Adre adovo shillopen:
And here's a thing I'd like to ask—
          Ko'll sikker mengy cavacoi
Why is the cruel winter sent?
          Sossi Miduvel kairs o wen?

'Under the snow the children sought,
          'I chavos rudered pre a lay
And found some sticks, just four or five:
          Ta latcher koshters tull' o yiv,
I made a fire of what they brought;
          Te mandy kaired o yag apre—
'Twas hard to keep the flame alive.
          Sos dusheri ta kair lis jiv.

'Already, do you mind, we had
       'Hookey, tu jins, amandi lelled
Three sons – enough to manage for:
       Trin chavos, sarja bockeli:
Well, on that very night, my lad,
       Adre adovo ratti welled,
The wife had twins—ay, two boys more!
       Dui waver tiknos, ketteni.

'The morning after came a gent—
       'Ovavo divvus welled a mush—
The Queen's head-gamekeeper, I knew:
       Sos I krallissas yagengro;
Said he: "How dare you stick your tent
       Ma hatch kekoomi "dre o wesh!"
Up here, you lazy Gipsy, you?
       Yuv pukked amengy, hunnalo."

'One of my little chaps called out:
       'Yeck, o'mi chavos shelled avri:
"Sir, won't you look a bit in there,
       "Rye, dick a wongish 'dre o tan—
And see the babies mother's got?—
       Dick yeckora, sa rinkeni
Such pretty little things they are!"
       I dui nevvi tiknos shan!"

'He put his head just half-way in:
       'Yuv chivved yuvs sherro pash adre
Ah, 'twas a cheerless sight he found –
       Ah, sos but dukkeri ta dick
My wife, poor dear, a-shiverin', –
       I juva, shillerin' dovalay,
The babies, born upon the ground.
       I tiknos, beeno 'pre o chick.

'He looked with pity in his eyes:
       'Sos kammoben 'dre lester yak:
"Twins, twins!" he cried—"why there you got
       "Dui, dui! pendas yuv aja;
Rather too much of a surprise,
       Adovo se too buti bak
My poor old fellow, did you not?"
       For tute—tacho, miro ba?"

'And when he turned and left us soon,
     'An' sa yuv pirried sig adrom,
"Twins, twins!" again I heard him say:
     "Dui, dui!" sos yuvs lastus lav.
Now listen: that same afternoon
     Adóvo se too büti bäk
A little light-cart came our way.
     For túte—tàcho, mïro bä?'

'The gamekeeper was driving it:
     'O yagengro sos toolin lis;
"Come on," he cried, "you've never seen
     "Rom, avacai!" yuv pukked aja,
A cart-load such as this, I bet—
     "Se chummeny kushto, dick a list,
And it's a present from the Queen.
     Sar bitchered fon I krallissa.

"She's heard what troubles you have had—
     "Yoi's shuned o'tiro dukkerben—
Your two poor babies, born in there,
     I dui chavos chivved acai;
And of your wife who's lying so bad,
     Acovos lakis delaben
So she has sent these things for her."
     For tiri chavos te I dye"

'Well, there was plenty in that cart:
     'Sos buti dre o wardo, pal:
A pair of blankets for my wife.
     Dui boro coppas—avali:—
Food, and a bottle full of port –
     Habben, yeck walin lullo mol –
God bless that Lady all her life!
     Miduvelest' I Ranis see!

'There were some clothes too, and between
     'Pash rinkeni heezis—shun kenna
Lay children's woollen stockings, those
     Sos buti tatti hovalos;
She'd knitted – she herself – the Queen,
     Yoi tivdas len—I krallissa—
The Lady of the Gorgios!
     I rani pre I Gorgios!

'The biggest children, all the three,
           'I boro chavos, sar I trin,
Put each a pair of stockings on;
           Rivved dovo bovalos apre:
They looked as pretty as could be,
           Yul dicked sa kushto, prasterin
Well shod, and trotting up and down.
           Sa rinkeni chukkered, pre a lay.

'Thought I: there's many a Gorgio –
           'Tacho, shan barvelo Gorgios,
Rich lords and ladies in the land,
           Buti, adre acove tem,
Who'd be uncommon proud to show
           Ko'd kam ta sikker hovalos
Socks knitted by the Queen's own hand.
           Tivved pa I Ranis noko fem.

'But for that Lady I'd have had
           'Ma kamli juva asti mer
To see my wife die over there;
           Bi moro Ranis delaben:
You needn't wonder, need you, lad,
           Tacho, mi kamava ta kair
That I'd do anything for her.
           Worisso, lakis kammoben.

'So if she wants a man to box,
           'If yoi kamel'a a mush ta koor,
I'll fight her battles, never fear! –
           Shom sar acai! Pal av aja –
'Twas dry work talking of them socks –
           Mukks pi a tas o'levinor
Let's drink the Queen's good health in beer.'
           For kam o'moro krallissa!'

ELI & GERT FRANKHAM

Eli Frankham and his wife Gert live in a village not far from King's Lynn. The surrounding countryside is flat, black fenland, mostly used for vegetable crops and scored by dykes. A passing postman, busy on his morning deliveries, directed me to their bungalow, and I was glad I had asked him because it would have been easy to have missed the opening to their short, winding drive. The postman must have known their entrance well, however, because over the years Eli has had much to do with procuring a fair deal for gypsies: he is president of the National Romany Rights Association, and in this capacity has fought in favour of gypsy living sites and education for gypsy children, causes which, I discovered, have even taken him abroad, and much of it work which is unpaid.

When I pulled up at the bungalow Gert was outside sorting potatoes: a tall, fine-looking woman, her good looks in fact belie her fragile health. She explained that Eli was out in a field repairing a fence; she didn't expect him to be long, so we went inside. Over coffee and large chocolate chip biscuits Gert told me that she had been married since 1953; her maiden name was Cole. Her father had been known as 'the wild man of Hampshire', a name immortalised on his impressive angel-topped stone in Winchester cemetery. 'It's because when he was drunk he'd go wild and fight bare-fisted – although he never touched us kids,' Gert explained.

Gert and Eli and (opposite) a striking couple on their wedding day

Eli came in. He is undoubtedly a man with presence, broad chested, with a dark moustache and around his neck the traditional Romany red neckerchief. With the ease of a natural storyteller he picked up the theme of names: 'I'm related to the Lees, the Mitchells, the Smiths and Loveridges, and of course the Frankhams. My great-great-grandfather was Hezekiah Frankham, and he had three sons: Jesse, William and Sam. They used to go round Hampshire and Sussex cutting crops by hand; Hezekiah would sit under a tree and sharpen their sickles. Farmers paid them one pound an acre, but one year when they got to a farm to cut a crop they said that they wanted a guinea – that's a shilling more – and refused to start. The next day the farmer rode up to them and said "Well, have you made your minds up, are you cutting or not? And be sure I've made my mind up, it's £99 for 99 acres, take it or leave it!" And with that he rode off. Of course, they had to take it.

'Not long afterwards they went to a pub called the Earl of March at Selsey. It was

Goodwood Races time, and there were a lot of horsedrawn cabs outside which had been doing business taking people to and from the course. The bar was crowded.' Eli paused here, then continued.

'Now, this is the story which has been handed down in the family: one of Hezekiah's sons bought him a drink, but when he looked for it on the counter it had gone; so the son bought him another, but that was taken, too. Well, a fight broke out, and great-grandfather was killed. He's buried in the churchyard two hundred yards from the pub, under the yew tree, and it's an open verdict to this day as to what happened. However, the landlord had been seen to lean over the bar and hit Hezekiah, and later he disappeared, suddenly and completely. There was talk of a horse-drawn van taking him down to a tin mine in Cornwall – but that might have been wild rumours; he probably went of his own accord, fearing reprisals. Certainly Hezekiah's sons were not men to fall out with.

George (left) and Jo Frankham leaving the boxing booths on Soton Common in the early 1920s

'Sam was a boxer. He'd go to a fair or a big meeting, push a stick in the ground and challenge anyone. He was also what was known as a "gentleman's fighter", because often a rich lord or dandie would find him an opponent and wager a purse – say, a hundred guineas – on Sam winning. It was bare-knuckle fighting. Sam was never beaten, and he'd get a share of the purse.'

Eli took a draught of coffee and then said: 'You know the introduction clip to all Top Rank films, the one which shows the muscleman beating the gong? Well, that was Bombadier Billie Wells, and Jo, Sam's son, beat Billie Wells for the British Empire title. Jo was born in a bender tent on Shedfield Common at Wickham, Hampshire. Sam died when he was thirty-four, and his wife married again, a man called Beckett; so Jo took the name Beckett, although he was really a Frankham.'

'Do you keep to the same family Christian names?' I asked.

'Yes, my grandfather was Eli, and my father, and so is my eldest son. Having said that, my great-grandfather was William. He married Mary, a Welsh travelling woman who drove a horse and cart and sold fish. But they had a boy born in 1873 and they called him Eli (my grandfather). They had a younger son, too, Jesse, born in 1892, and he was awarded the Croix de Guerre, the French Cross of War in the Great War. He was dressed up as a German officer and went on horseback behind the German lines to spy. He went down one flank and up the other and all the men saluted him, but when he headed back towards his own lines the Germans shot his horse from under him. He scrambled from shell hole to shell hole until he reached the French lines.

(right) Eli's grandfather and his brother-in-law and (below) The flower stall in Charlotte Street, Portsmouth

'My grandfather, Eli, he fought in the Boer War.' Eli gets up and fetches from an adjoining room a framed photo of two men in uniform, grandfather Eli and his brother-in-law, who also fought in the Boer War.

'Grandfather was heavyweight champion of the Royal Hampshire Regiment,' Eli says as we study the two soldiers. 'And my father, Eli, he could box, too. He fought an Irishman called "Devil Skin" (Edward) Ayres in Lord Selborne's meadow early one morning in 1923, when he was only young. It was a barefisted fight, and Ayres was a big, thick-skinned, dark man. It was hop-picking time, and a lot of local travellers gathered round. Ella Loveridge and Jack Locke were there – at the time my father was courtin' my mother, who was their grand-daughter, Rosie Saunders.

'Great-grandad Jack Locke was a wicked man – he used to knock Ella about. She was a brave woman. She had a son called Ballo, and poor Ballo was wounded and blinded in World War I. Ella got permission to go from Bristol to France, and walked down the Red Cross hospital lines: she shouted out "Ballo!" and he called out, "Here I am, my mum!" And she sat down beside him and he died in her arms.

'I wrote a poem about mothers once,' Eli said, looking reflective; 'I think you've got to

express yourself with feeling in poetry and music. Mind you,' he added with a twinkle, 'the mother is the guv'nor of every big family!'

We talked about his own mother, Rose Saunders. Eli: 'Her parents were Tommy and Valence (Providence Locke) and they had a flower stall in Charlotte Street in Portsmouth. It was opposite the pub called The Empress of India, and was the first in a line of stalls which went down the street. They sold flowers raised by local growers, and I remember catching a bus with Grannie to Purbrook just outside Portsmouth to gather coloured ivies; I'd climb the trees and throw bunches of ivy down. We used to gather moss on the downs around Cosham, too, and we'd bring the greenery back in sacks on the bus; what Grannie didn't sell off the stall she'd sell to her relatives, the Deacons, who had flower shops in Portsmouth.

'Grannie and Grandad had lots of relations. One of them, Jimmy Guest, used to keep donkeys for rides on the seafront. He was only a tiny man and his two sons became jockeys over the sticks. There's still jockeys in the family.

'Grandad had some stables near the flower stall, and I'd go out with him to the country to cut grass for the horse. I remember one day when we were out he came over ill, sweating and collapsing. I had to get him home, and then he was ill for weeks; it was the after-effects of the mustard gas he'd been subjected to in the trenches.

'He had a sad life. One day during the war he'd come back behind the lines for a rest, and one of the other soldiers was reading a newspaper from home. This chap said, "Well, that's bad luck – there's a poor bloke out here fighting for king and country, and his child's been burnt to death." Grandfather couldn't read or write, so he asked, "Where's that, mate?" And the chap said "Landport Street, Portsmouth; Sally Saunders – her pinafore caught fire, and her mum dragged her out into the yard under the tap, but it was no good."

'Sally was my mother's older sister. Grandad walked out to No Man's Land, and they had to call him back. And then when the poor old fellow came out of the army, his twin boys – who always dressed the same, in old gypsy clothes – they were walking along the street and a big wall crumbled and fell on them, and killed them outright. They were ten or eleven at the time.'

Eli's mother, Rose Saunders (standing), and his younger sister Emma

Although it's over sixty years since Tommy Saunders died, it is obvious that he left a lasting impression on Eli: 'He was a gentleman; never swore in his life. His favourite food was hedgehog, and every morning he had a pound of steak. If he saw a tramp out of the workhouse he'd give him money for a cup of tea, and he'd say to his wife, "Valence, where's me supper?" and then he'd give some to the tramp.'

By this time, with Eli in full flow, Gert had moved off to busy herself with jobs around the kitchen. Their daughter and her boyfriend had come in for lunch; they'd been doing the fencing which Eli would have been doing were he not inside with me, reminiscing. Happy that the fencing was progressing well enough without him, Eli continued:

'Before the war Grandad Saunders and his family lived in a horse-drawn waggon, but when he went away Portsmouth Corporation housed Grannie and the children and saw to it that the children went to school. That was how my mother learned to read and write. She thought it was a good thing, and so when I was school age she sent me to school in Horndean. At the time Dad had bought a field in Fiveheads Road, and we lived in a waggon there.

'I was the only gypsy in the school, and the other kids used to call out "Gippo, Gippo!" I had a rough time. I used to fight, and I used to play hookey but my mother didn't know.

'Through playing hookey I fell in with another boy called Marshall. There was a lot of empty property about in those days, and we broke into an empty house. Marshall, who lived in a house, said to me "See that box?" – it was a gas meter – "There's money in it," he said. I'd never seen a gas meter before, but he prised it open. In fact there was nothing in it, but someone saw us and we'd done 7s 6d worth of damage. Of the two of us, I was made to take the blame. The authorities said I was "out of parental control", even though mother had wrapped my sandwiches up each day thinking I was going in to school. I was sent to an approved school in Southampton, and was locked in a room for a week – but I escaped, and was on the run for two or three days. I was ten years old.

'The authorities wanted to send me to Wales, but Mother and Father said it was too far to visit, and so they sent me to the National Children's Home and Orphanage in Alexander Road, Farnborough. There were two or three hundred boys there, and do you know, they had a very good band. The bandmaster was H. P. Lovell, and he looked at me and said, "I think you'd make a fine musician!" So he put me on a cornet, and I became the one and only, number one cornet player! We made records, and H. P. Lovell taught me all the great pieces of music. He composed, too. His friend was Kenneth J. Alfred who wrote the regimental march "Colonel Bogey". Alfred had written it for a competition, and H. P. Lovell entered the same competition with his "Young Courageous". In fact Lovell won, and

A young Eli

received a gold watch and £50. Kenneth J. Alfred's "Colonel Bogey" came second, and he had a silver watch and chain and £25.' Eli paused, and through a series of da, da, da, das, gave me a burst of both tunes: they were similar.

He continued, 'I was in the children's home nearly four years, and when I came out Father bought me a cornet and I continued to play. Even when I was called up into the army, although I was a signalman, I did a stint as a bugler at one time because there wasn't one in the regiment!'

Eli then slipped a cassette into a player and pressed the start button, and the words and music which emanated from it were quite beautiful. The piece was called 'Opre Roma' ('Arise Gypsy'), and he'd written it himself: 'I just picked up the pen to do it,' he said simply.

He is a man of many parts: for instance, in the army he had continued the Frankham tradition in boxing, and at one time had become the Middle East Land Forces middleweight champion. Boxing hadn't been entirely new to him, however:

'Just before I was called up I'd started to box for Sam McCowan who had a booth on Southampton Common. He was a well known Cornish showman. Freddie Mills came off his booth. You fought in boxing gloves and people would come and watch, several hundred people. If you could go several rounds you'd get 30s for half an hour. That was "knobbins", collected with a hat; and if it was a good show you'd get another couple of quid.

'When I came out of the army in 1948 I boxed in the booths again. Sometimes Sam would "plant" me in the crowd as a "volunteer" in case they couldn't get anybody to come up and fight. Then I became a professional. Nat Sellars was my manager – he managed Freddie Mills – and my trainer was my godfather Edwin Penfold who'd been middleweight champion for the West of England.

'I stopped fighting when I married Gert – though we Romanies still have what we call "grudge fights". In fact there was one early the other morning – something sparked it off and the only way to settle it was bare fists, a bit of blood, a broken nose and a couple of teeth missing, followed by a handshake!'

GERT'S STORY

'My mother is eighty-six. She lives in Swindon, and still does her own cooking and cleaning. This Christmas I went to look after her, but she ended up looking after me – oh, and she made twelve or fourteen dozen paper flowers for Christmas!

'She had a hard upbringing. She was a Smith, and her own mother died young, leaving small children. I ring my mum every night, we're not like mother and daughter. Since I was six I always went out with her, and later on my own, callin' with the baskets. I've still got my baskets.

'We were living in a bender tent at Winchester [similar to that shown in the photograph above] when she was ill with the youngest one, and I had to earn enough money to pay for medicine for her. I'd go callin', make paper flowers, do farm work. I was thirteen, and I used to go off on the train; it was thruppence from Basingstoke to Reading, half fare. I'd beg for woollens and rags to sell, and if I earnt a quid I was doing well. At 3 o'clock I'd ask at the bread shop for a sackful of cakes (their earliest bake) and get some bread, too; at that time you could get a loaf for sixpence. Then I'd buy a pennyworth of cheese. When I got off the train my brother Willie met me and we'd walk two miles home. Then I'd do the cooking – Dad wouldn't make even a cup of tea! The baby was called Michael. I had four brothers and one sister; Willie was the eldest.

'Dad dealt in horses, but never went to Appleby. We did all the Hampshire fairs: Wickham and the New Forest, and he went to Reading Block Horse Sales the first Friday in every month. I'd ride one of the horses back from the fair.

'Sometimes on a Saturday or Sunday afternoon we'd get on the flat trolley and go out to visit someone. But we were never allowed to ask them for bread or a drink, and always had to call people "Uncle" and "Aunt" even if we'd never seen 'em before. I still do if I see old travellers; it's a mark of respect.

'I can remember back to when I was five years old. Then, if we had a big fire outside and we'd met up with other families, we weren't allowed to go to their fires. But 75 per cent of the time we were on our own – even after being married for over forty years, we're still on our own. When I was a kid, men and women used to get round the fire, and if Dad gave a certain look, we children had to melt away; and if women were talking about babies, we weren't allowed to listen!

'When I was twelve or fourteen, me and me brother Willie used to go out in the woods and carry wood out, and saw it into loads of logs with a bowsaw, then drive out with Dad and sell it.

'Me and Willie used to go out ferritin' for rabbits. It might be ice and snow and I'd be shivering, but daren't talk in case the rabbits heard and they'd lay in the burrow and not come out. We used to sell the rabbits for one and thruppence [6p] to butchers. We used to knock doors, too, and ask "Have you got a couple of skins?" They knew we meant rabbits, and might say: "Yes, but you'll have to skin the rabbits – and then they'd bring them, and we used to stand at the door and do it. Me brother taught me how, but he wouldn't teach me to make clothes pegs because it was down and out work we'd been raised on, and he didn't want me to do it. We also used to ask for rags and scrap. If we got scrap, Dad would come for it with the horse and trolley. We worked hard; my brother used to say to me, "You shouldn't do any work when you get married, Sis, you've done your work." '

I asked how she and Eli had met. Eli answered: 'I'd come out of the army and was working with my father. He was living in a bender tent. We gathered moss for Covent Garden wreathmaking, and herbs for medicine companies. We did farm work, too. You see, farmers gave gypsies menial tasks that no one wanted – who better to ask than gypsies, who had their own homes and were no bother? It was all going into one pocket with gypsies, though. One of the land jobs was pulling sugar beet.'

Gert joined in, and explained beet pulling: 'A horse-drawn plough would loosen the beet – only as much as you could do in a day – and you'd pull 'em out of the ground, then knock two together to get the soil off, and lay 'em in rows, six rows to a line; then you'd come back down the rows and chop the green leaves off with a "greyhound" knife. It was called that because the blade was thin and long. You'd put the leaves back over them to protect them from the frost.'

The 'greyhound' knife which Gert used to use for trimming sugar beet and (opposite) this photo was taken when Eli was filmed for a television programme

Eli: 'Well, one particular day a farmer offered Father and me £8 an acre for beeting in a field near Wickham, but we thought that wasn't enough money and said "No". Later in the day I was with my brother-in-law, in an Austin 7 I had then, and we went by the field and I said, "There's some gypsies doing what we left." It was Gert and her brother, and it was teeming with rain – they were like drowned rats. But I noticed Gert and said, "What a pretty girl."

'At that time Dad had moved from the bender and we were living in a railway carriage on a farm at Wickham. I remember Gert came to meet my sisters there, but I saw her, too – and I was good-looking and she took a shine to me and we got courtin'! She was seventeen and I was about twenty-eight when we married.

'After we married Gert went out callin' and I did forestry work in Kent. At first we travelled with a horse and tent, then we got a caravan.'

Eli then told the following extraordinary tale of another van, an old showman's waggon he'd bought in Kent. It came from a man called 'Huppty-Back George' and had stood for years in George's farm milkyard at Headcorn.

Eli: 'In its day this van would have been pulled by six horses. It had a set of heavy iron wheels, and was like a mansion inside; there was a door in the centre and windows each side, and big steps up to the door. I had it as an office, but although it had a bit of a cold feeling inside, Gert said, "It's so nice let's sleep in it!" Now at the time I had a dog called Rover, a

Johnnie Frankham, former British Lightweight Boxing Champion, is related to both Eli and Gert

good guard dog which barked if there were strangers about at night; I knew its bark for someone we knew. The dog lay at the bottom of the steps on a mat, and we go into the caravan to sleep.

'Late in the night a loud knocking woke us. I looked out, but Rover looked up at me surprised, and I realised he hadn't heard anything. I knew then the caravan was haunted. I said to Gert, "Guess what – tocklum!" – that means haunted. She just said, "Go back to sleep."

'Next night I kept my trousers on ready, and at 12.30 there was the same loud "bang, bang". I came down the steps and checked the jacks on the trailer … nothing.

'We brought the van back to Stockbridge and Gert's brother Jimmie said he'd like to buy the cushions and mirrors, and another chap called Smudger Smith said he'd like the cut-glass windows. But I said "No, you can buy the whole waggon" and I sold the whole lot to Smudgie – but didn't tell him about the knockin'!

'Smudgie pulled the waggon into his yard and an old bloke called Bert who worked for him slept in it. However, at 12.30, the knockin' came. The old boy shouted out "Stop your boys knocking the caravan, I've got to get up for work in the morning!" Smudger shouted back "They're here in bed", and Smudger's two dogs never stirred. After three nights the old man left.

'Then Smudgie's wife 'Omie [Naomi] said to him, "Let's sleep up there, it's lovely!" So they put the bedding in. And at 12.30 the knockin' came. She remembered what the old man had said, and they both rushed out shivering and shaking.

'Smudge sold it to an old man known as "Bull Bread"; he lived in an old tin hut in a yard. He decorated the waggon all up, and painted it; it took him three months to do it, and to renew all the tin on it. Then he destroyed his hut and moved in. He had two nights in it – and then burnt it to the ground with diesel and petrol. As it burnt, the most horrible screams came from it as if someone was being burnt to death. And when the old man was clearing up the bits, he found over half a pound in weight of gold in a heap in the hub of a wheel – it had probably been gold coins. You see, there had been something, someone, between the wood and the thick outside tin of the van, knocking and telling us to strip it down.'

Eli tells a good tale, and everyone in the bungalow kitchen, who'd been helping themselves to a huge plate of sandwiches Gert had made, had paused spellbound as he talked. We now all finished up to the last crumb. Eli made ready to go out with his daughter and her boyfriend to finish the fencing. Gert was going to drive to a fair at Horseman's Den in Kent, and I had the long journey home in front of me. However, before I left Eli asked me if I'd help him to find a horse he hadn't seen since the 1930s!

'A big, strong, lovely 15.2hh black horse called Punch which used to pull our "Reading" vardo when I was a boy,' he explained. 'My grandfather "Squire" Frankham sold Punch to Lord and Lady Woolavington of Graffham Park, Midhurst, and he used to pull the milk float from the estate to the station. Now, Lord and Lady Woolavington had two Derby winners; "Captain Cuttle" in 1922, and "Coronach" in 1926, and they had them stuffed and put in big glass cases. When Punch died, Lady Woolavington had him stuffed, too! She must have loved that horse! Well, I'd like to see him again if you can help me find him.'

I promised I'd do my best, though at the present time we're still searching. Eli sends me letters on his National Romany Rights notepaper. The logo on the paper is the association's name encircling two crossed clothes pegs – the pegs were Eli's idea. He's definitely a man of many parts!

The Evil Eye

A Gloucestershire farming couple speaking in recent times of a
neighbouring farmer:

'He wouldn't sell a gypsy named Smith a truss of hay and Smith said to
him: "You'll die in a ditch." Less than a fortnight afterwards he did.
He had a hunting accident. The gypsy put a grudge on him.'

HARRIET HALL

The last time I met Harriet she was breathless through the effects of asthma, but in spite of her disability, she had the kettle on the gas ring and her caravan door open in readiness for my visit. When I approached, her little black dog Sooty barked from his kennel beside the caravan, and Harriet herself came to the door, her lean face lit with smiles. She is thin with the frailness of someone who has worn their body away with work over the years, and the hands preparing the tea with tinned milk – a sensible commodity when the shops are miles away, and you are without the luxury of a refrigerator – look work-worn, too.

Harriet has lived in her caravan, tucked away in a corner of a farmer's field, for over thirty years. In fact she has two caravans, the other within stepping distance and slightly larger; but most of the year she spends in the small one, an 'Eccles', with an ivory watersilk pattern to the melamine cupboard and drawer fronts. She has a coal fire and a Calor gas stove, and hopes that one day electricity will be laid on. Her son Harry has succeeded in having the caravan connected to the telephone.

On the first occasion that I had met Harriet I'd met Harry, too; it was near to Christmas, and he and his wife Eileen had come to collect moss from nearby for wreath-making – the previous year they'd made half an acre of wreaths, and sold them to a flower shop. The only thing they buy for a wreath is the foundation, and that is because it would take too long to make.

Harry is clever and good-looking, and has Harriet's bright blue eyes. A true gypsy, he can turn his hand to anything, and despite never learning to read or write (more of which later), can make an adequate job of building, motor maintenance, market gardening, tree-lopping, plumbing, electrical work, cooking, looking after livestock, and flower- and wreath-making. At the time he was wreath-making he was also selling catering vans.

We'd talked of vans generally, and Harriet had declared that when she died she wanted her caravans burnt, Romany fashion. Harry, his interest in motors to the fore, joked that it would be a waste, particularly of the Eccles which he would advertise in a motor magazine – and in fact he knew of a man who collected them, and had five so far. Despite this, Harriet will probably get her wish: when Isaac, Harry's father, died, Harriet had overseen the burning of the Eccles caravan they then had. It had weighed four tons empty, had cut-glass windows and was worth £25,000, but they had melted it down, and Harriet's other son Ike (Isaac) had cut up the remaining chassis and put it into a presser.

Opposite: Harriet Hall

The £25,000 trailer which was burnt when Hodge died

Harry and Ike are the only boys of Harriet's seven children. Her daughters – Evelyn, Priscilla, Shirley, Mary and Norma – are all married with their own homes. Their father died one Christmas Day from a heart attack. He came home slightly the worse for drink, started to play his melodeon, and collapsed. Harry explained that his father had had heart disease from smoking, but had neglected it instead of going to a doctor for treatment. Harriet recollected that in October he had dreamed, strangely, about his funeral, describing how he had seen two lorries carrying flowers – and on the funeral day there had indeed been two. Harriet called him 'Old Hodge', for that had been his nickname – even the children called him 'Hodge'.

On the next occasion I met Harriet she was on her own, and we talked about her childhood, where hardship was no stranger:

'I never really knew who my father was. My mother, who is ninety-six and still looking after herself, told me that when she was twenty-six she went with her horse and flat dray to Burton-on-Trent to collect enamel pastry bowls and buckets from a factory there; but by the time she got near the place it was getting dark, and because she had no lights on the cart she pulled in and put a bit of sheet down and slept under the dray. And that night she was raped by Jack Smith, a married man commonly known as Blackguard Jack.

'After I was born I lived with mother and my grandparents – in fact, that's how I began smoking, when I was just two! Great-grandfather was blind, and he would lean over the doors at the back of the waggon so's I could light his pipe with a piece of flaming newspaper.' Harriet added, 'I smoked up until two years ago, but you know, I've gone worsener with me breath since I stopped.'

She went on: 'When I was 4½, Mum married a man called Smith who'd been born on Bentley Common near Solihull. He'd go out with a pony and cart and get scrap, rags, and bags of old harness; by repairing old bridles and stuffing padding into collars he'd make up new sets from the old harness.

'Mum had eight children by Mr Smith, and being the oldest child I stopped at the camp and looked after the others. There was a set of twins, called Lily and Lizabeth, so identical that you could only tell the difference between them because Lily had a dog bite which marked her upper lip.

'I did all the washing, boiling up the water in a ten-gallon pot which I hung onto a kettle iron. I used to enjoy it – boil the tea-towels first, then bedsheets and then the kids' underclothes. And I also looked after thirty-six horses tethered on ropes, and saw to their watering, and scrubbed out three horse-drawn caravans a day. At other times in the day I'd help Step-dad make pegs and flowers; in summer I didn't know what it was to sit down! I was allowed five whole cigarettes a week, and Step-father's dog ends.'

Harriet then opened a drawer and brought out a worn knife, the bottom half of its handle rounded like the bottom of a figure-eight: 'It's my peg knife! I made it years ago – the handle's yew, the furrell's a bit of copper water pipe, and the blade's from an old knife. I use this to split a piece of withy wood to "mouth it" so that you get the two ends to grip the washing onto the line.' She cradled the knife in her hands and I photographed it. As I put the camera away Harriet made more tea, then carried on talking.

'When I was fifteen Step-father bought me a Bradford Open-Lot waggon; he got it for £60 from Mr Sambrooks of Brownhills. When I got together with 'Odge [Isaac Hall] he only had the clothes he stood up in, but I had a horse-drawn waggon and the harness to go with it! Four could sleep on the top where the bed was, and four under that bed, and there was space for a mattress on the floor in front.'

Harriet went on to tell how she'd known Hodge for some time because he'd come to live with their group as a friend, and she related how in his early life he'd known tragedy: 'His father drowned in the canal at Tipton. It was near Christmas time, and he'd been carrying bags of oranges and nuts for his children's Christmas stockings. The bags were found beside the canal bridge wall. His family believed that a traveller had a grudge against him and pushed him in, but nothing was ever proved, and even after seventy years it's still an open verdict.'

Harriet admitted that it was obvious from when he first started living with them that Hodge didn't like going out to work: 'He preferred to stay with the waggon and do chores like washing. But he was spotlessly clean, and you'd never find a dirty tea-towel.'

Harriet displays her peg knife

Whilst Hodge stayed home, Harriet went out to work every day on a milk-float pulled by her pony Peggy. She loved Peggy, having raised her on a 'titty' bottle. She said of the work: 'I got the name "The Tatter" because as well as selling our home-made pegs and flowers, I collected rags. Before I went out I'd load the float with a tankful of goldfish, some plastic flying birds on bits of elastic, and boxes of small live chickens. The fish, six or seven hundred, came from Mr Coley of Greybray Road, Wolverhampton. The chickens, also about seven hundred of them, used to cost me £1 10s [£1.50] for a hundred. They'd have just hatched out of incubators so I'd have to keep 'em warm at night. I used to give either the chickens, flying birds or fish in exchange for rags. The fish I'd scoop out of the tank with a ladle into jamjars or bowls which the mums or their kids brought out. People got to know my horse and cart, and the little kids would call out "Hey up, Peggy's coming, better get her a bit of bread or a carrot!"

'I used to take the rags to a marime stores where they were tied up into big bales. For general rags I'd get £3 a hundredweight. These went to Manchester to go into presses to make paper. For "wipers", which were things like old blouses and sheets, I'd get £7 a hundredweight. Garages bought them from the stores.

'I usually only bought rags and wipers, but one day a woman I knew came out with two little vases and asked me to buy them. I said, "You'll have nothing left in the house," but she was desperate for money to feed her children, she'd seen more mealtimes than meals. I gave her some money, and I've kept the little vases to this day.'

Harriet told me that six of her children were born in the family's horse-drawn living waggon. Harry was born at ten o'clock one November night when they were driving back from Pershore; Hodge had to pull in by a canal, and then went to a farm to phone for a midwife. However, she had her last child in hospital, because as she explained: 'I didn't want my daughters to have to do the dirty washing.'

She would take her children with her when she went out with the milk-float, putting the youngest in a high seat in the front. 'We'd take sandwiches, bottles of pop and a flask of tea; sometimes we'd be given a jug of tea. When I got home I'd give the kids something to eat, then get peg-wood ready to put the tin on. Then I'd fetch me own water, bathe the kids and put them to bed. After that I'd tidy up, and often at three or four o'clock in the morning I'd be putting washing on the line.'

Harriet had a brief respite from work when her daughter Shirley was born: 'I didn't go out at first on me rounds because it's unlucky for a woman to go to a house without the child having been baptised or the woman having been "churched". My brother-in-law, who lived nearby, brought a tank of a hundred goldfish and a box of a hundred chickens and said to Big 'Odge, could he take them and catch the kids coming out of school at Great Wyrley, and told him to get the pony harnessed.

'Now, with the pony I could talk to it just like a bebby and she'd do anything for me – I only had to whistle and she'd come. But when 'Odge approached her she got fierce, opened her mouth to bite and backed off. Me brother-in-law was in stitches. 'Odge said, "No way, I'm not

Opposite: Harriet and her waggon

40

doing it!" It was a Monday, and that very day I'd been up the village and got Shirley baptised, she'd still got her pink ribbons on. I plonked the baby's bottle down by 'Odge, and I told him that the other children needed feeding, too. Then I harnessed Peggy and managed to get rid of the fish and chickens in an hour.'

Harriet explained to me that they had come to the district in which she now lives because there was farm work to be had. 'I'd send the children off up the field and 'Odge would go with them – but when I got there 'Odge's hoe would be under the hedge, and I'd say to the children "Where is he?" – and they'd say he'd gone off to visit so-and-so.'

Although Hodge did not relish farm work, Harry, Harriet's son, had found favour with a farmer who wanted him to look after his deep-litter broilers. Harry was nine at the time, and never went to school because the farmer wanted him working full-time – when school inspectors came round, the farmer told them that Harry had come from some distance away and was only passing through. And Harriet was frightened to cross the farmer in case he put them off his land.

I later learned from Harry that his non-attendance at school left a legacy which hurts: because he cannot read or write, other members of the family have to read things for him and they call him stupid – only in fun, of course, but he doesn't like it, particularly as he knows that if he had been literate he could have got a job as an engineer which he would have loved – evidently he is so good with engines that the local car mechanic comes to him for advice!

At the time Harry also told me that he doesn't drink because he saw too much of his father coming home drunk and hitting Harriet. He and his brother and sisters used to go to bed with their coats on, because when Hodge came back from the pub he'd throw them and Harriet out of the waggon. Harriet admitted that one day after being particularly badly beaten she had harnessed the horse and cart and, taking the children with her, covered the 35-mile journey to her mum and step-dad in a day.

Harriet told me that when Peggy, her beloved horse, was eighteen, Hodge sold her and used the money to buy a motor van. The Open-Lot waggon went to a museum in Worcester. Harriet was so upset over losing Peggy that she had a nervous breakdown and went down to 4½ stone in weight. It was at this time that she spotted a monkey for sale in the local pet shop: each time she went to town she went to look at it, and longed to have it – but it cost £25.

'I went on and on about it, and then one day I was out with our Shirley and Harry, and his dad came down the street with a box: "Oh!" I said, "You've got the monkey! … But you ain't given me enough money to get it some nuts and bananas!" The kids said, "We'll get some from the pictures tonight." When we got into the lorry I didn't get into the front, I got into the back because I wanted to peep into the box. And there wasn't a monkey inside, there was two cats – one tabby, and one black-and-white: 'Odge had bought 'em from the pet shop for half-a-crown apiece. 'Odge said: "An old-fashioned traveller wanting a monkey – never heard the like!"

'One of the cats was in kitten. I loved them and looked after them, and lots more stray cats from around and about used to come to me – at one time I had fifty-three!'

If life between Hodge and Harriet wasn't exactly a bed of roses, Harriet's last story confirms that she was match enough for him when the occasion demanded: 'Big 'Odge loved his birds. He had fifteen hens and two cocks, and he used to keep them in runs – but one day when I came back from work he'd loosed them out and there was muck everywhere. I threatened that I'd pull their necks if it happened again. But he let them out every day. Then there came a time when he went away for a week, and I took them up into the field and left them. They laid eggs all over the place, and as the days went by they got less and less as the fox took 'em.

'When he came home he said "Our Harriet, where's me hens?" Harriet's thin face lights up and she laughs wickedly at this memory.

Whilst Harriet was telling this story, Dave, the tractor driver from the farm, called in on his way home from work. Harriet, having done land work for years, knows him well and was quick with a cup of tea for him. She is a kind and generous person, and it was through her kindness to a friend of mine that we'd first met. I'm glad we did. I feel that as long as she's in her little caravan there'll be a welcome for me, and I can sit and hear her sprinkle her tales with phrases like: 'She'd skin a gnat's eye for a ha'penny' and, 'I'll spit black if that's not the truth!'

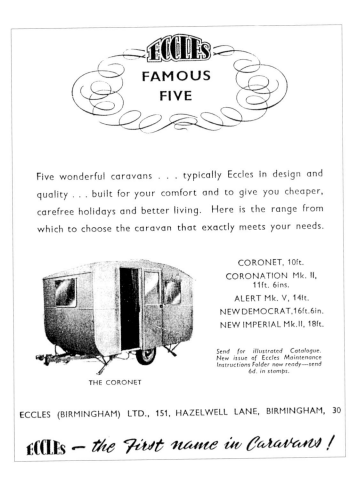

Joanna Clarke

THE GYPSY'S FOSTERLING

Whilst researching in Gloucester Records Office I was directed towards a very odd story: one of their efficient assistants, knowing that I was looking up references to gypsies, showed me a book and suggested I read the last chapter in it, because 'not many people know about it'. It had been written by Sybella Mary Crawley Boevey, and published about the turn of the century. I subsequently found out that Sybella was part of a family whose ancestors had lived for generations at Flaxley Abbey in the Forest of Dean. Her book was called *Dene Forest Sketches*, and it had a preface in which Sybella stated that the stories had 'a groundwork of truth …' and had been taken 'mainly from a mass of family papers, which are still hoarded at Flaxley like old gold'.

There was a brief reference to the background of each story, and of the last one, *The Gipsy's Fosterling*, she wrote that it was 'entirely founded on family letters and papers – two of the former (one in the time of the Great Plague) and given verbatim, and the chief characters are described from their portraits at Flaxley.' Turning to the back of the book, I read *The Gipsy's Fosterling* for myself, and was so enthralled by the strange coincidences in it that I found it difficult to believe it had a basis of truth.

I did some research. It appeared that the Boevey family had sold Flaxley Abbey some time ago; however, a branch of the family – that is, the great-great-great-nieces of Sybella – still lives locally. I spoke to both, first Margaret, then Pattie: Margaret referred me to Pattie whom she said knew more about history, and who opens Flaxley church each day. Pattie, who is a farmer, knew the book but hadn't read it for some time; she revealed that Sybella had been one of ten and had lived at home, and that the illustrations in the book had been done by her brother Arthur. I suggested that the facts within *The Gipsy's Fosterling* story seemed too extraordinary to be true, but Pattie said that Sybella was of a very moral, upright character, and that if she had written they'd been taken from family papers, then it was likely to be true.

I asked if I could quote the story and Pattie kindly said she couldn't see any objection, added to which it was probably long since out of copyright! So here is a shortened version.

THE GIPSY'S FOSTERLING

In the 1650s Flaxley Abbey was owned by two Dutch merchants: James and William Boeve. James had recently married Isabella de Visscher and spent little time at Flaxley; in fact, the place was left for the most part in the care of the two brothers' widowed sister, Joanna Clarke, who lived there with her small son Abraham.

The story opens with the two brothers away on business and Isabella staying with Joanna at Flaxley. The two sisters-in-law were as different as chalk and cheese, Isabella fashionable and worldly, Joanna quiet and puritan, even to her dress. Finding it difficult to entertain Isabella, Joanna suggested a walk up to the woods on nearby Welshbury Hill. During the walk they come across a gypsy encampment. The oldest of the gypsy women, a withered, thin creature called Nora Cree, asks to tell their fortune. Joanna declines, but Isabella gives the crone a copper and offers her hand.

Joanna draws aside and waits by a tree. Whilst stood there, she sees playing with other gypsy children a pretty little girl with blonde hair and blue eyes. The girl's looks make her stand out amongst the dark heads and faces of the others. Joanna looks longingly at the little girl, regretting that she never had a daughter. After a time Isabella, evidently unhappy with her fortune, snatches her hand away from Nora Cree, but before the two sisters-in-law move off, Joanna asks Nora the name of the little blonde girl and if they will be camped at Welshbury for a day or two. Nora tells her the girl's name is Nelly but is evasive as to the length of time they will be there.

The following day Isabella busies herself with packing, because she was leaving to join her husband. With Isabella occupied, Joanna took the opportunity to go back to the gypsy camp. Her small son Abraham, hoping to get his fortune told, went with her. The tents were still there and a few gypsies, but Nora Cree was not. Disappointed, for it was she

Flaxley Abbey

that Joanna wanted to speak to, she made her way back – but suddenly, en route, the woman appeared. After a few words Joanna asked after the little fair-haired girl Nelly, and Nora said she was out begging for no one could resist her; her face was worth a fortune to them.

Joanna guessed that the gypsies had stolen Nelly and might be uneasy about the deed, then proposed to Nora that if Nelly were handed to her to train as a personal attendant, she would give Nora ten pounds and no more questions would be asked about the girl. But Nora wouldn't make a decision. Meanwhile Abraham, Joanna's son, had taken the opportunity to scurry back to the gypsy camp, and now returned to his mother full of the news that he'd had his fortune told by a gypsy there and she'd said he would marry a girl with blue eyes and live in a big house and have lots of money!

A few weeks passed and nothing came of Joanna's offer to Nora Cree. Then one day whilst she was out in the abbey grounds, Joanna saw the little girl Nelly coming towards her, quite alone; when she reached Joanna she handed a note to her. It read: 'Put the gold behind the big tombstone outside the south wall of the church. If not there by moonrise tonight, the girl will be taken away. Look well to Eleanor Wiseman.'

Joanna crept out that evening and put the money by the tomb. From thence on, Nelly became a part of the household at Flaxley Abbey, and eventually a maidservant there.

Years passed and Abraham, now a young man, spent time living away, sometimes at Gloucester and sometimes in London with his Uncle James Boeve and Aunt Isabella. Joanna hoped that in London he would meet and eventually marry a suitable young society lady, and towards this end James and Isabella took him to various society functions.

However, at one such soirée it was Isabella, and not Abraham, who made an unsettling encounter. She was sitting on the outskirts of the crowded room when she was approached by a woman who introduced herself as Anne Aylway, and reminded her that she had been a friend of Isabella's sister Eleanor when they were girls. She asked Isabella for tidings of Eleanor, but Isabella replied: 'I can tell you nothing … she made a marriage disapproved of by her family, and we have had no communication with her for some time.'

Opposite: Flaxley Church, rebuilt in Victorian times, where the money was left by '… the big tombstone'

Mrs Aylway then told her that she had heard that Eleanor was living in London in great distress and poverty, and asked Isabella to stretch out a helping hand to her own sister. It was a plea to which Isabella made no reply. Oddly enough, Anne Aylway had her own connections with Flaxley Abbey: the owners of the estate before the Boeves had been a family called Kingston, and Peter Aylway, a relative of Anne's had married Annie Kingston in 1636.

Back at Flaxley, Nelly the servant girl had grown into a beautiful young woman and Joanna, seeing that Abraham was attracted to her, became increasingly anxious that he should stay up in London and find himself a suitable wife. She decided to go to London to oversee such matters herself.

She did go to London, but not for that reason. Word came that her brother William was dying, and her other brother James sent for her to go to London if not in time to see William, at least to be in time to attend his funeral. Meanwhile, James hastened to his brother's bedside. Mr John Langley, the minister of the Dutch church in London, was also present and had spent some time alone with William before James entered. When James approached William's bed his brother seemed very agitated and gasped to him 'Bell – deceived you – not the only daughter. Ask Anne Aylway.' These were his last words.

At the time of his death, William was sole owner of Flaxley Abbey and in his will he left Flaxley to Joanna; other relatives were remembered, though James received nothing, William stating that James's wife Isabella had brought him money. It was a bitter blow to Isabella, who by extravagant living had acquired large debts and was hoping that a legacy from William would settle them.

Joanna had brought her maidservant Nelly to London with her, and on seeing Nelly again, Abraham's passion for her was rekindled. His mother wasn't blind to the state of affairs, but obviously any match between Abraham and a servant was out of the question, and Joanna hastily took Nelly back to Flaxley.

On their return, the housekeeper Mrs Bunce informed Joanna that a man had come to the house and asked for her; he had said that Nora Cree was dying, and wanted Joanna to go to her at the camp on Welshbury. At first the name Nora Cree meant nothing to Joanna – then she remembered the first time she had seen Nelly at the gypsy camp, and old Nora telling Isabella's fortune.

Early the following morning she set off for the camp. Nora was in a small tent pitched apart from the others; the local minister Richard Hazell was with her, but he rose to wait outside when Joanna entered. She bent over the dying woman. In a state of anxiety Nora asked after Nelly, and Joanna assured her that the girl was safe and well. Then feebly Nora told her that it wasn't she, Nora, who had sold Nelly to her, but her son who wanted the ten pounds Joanna had offered. She then confirmed that the gypsies had stolen Nelly from a lady in London; she had been three or four at the time. They knew the name of her mother: it was Eleanor Wiseman, and when she'd been stolen she had been wearing a little gold locket. However, because it would have given away her identity, the gypsies had taken the locket from Nelly, although they couldn't sell it for fear of questions being asked. Over the years Nora had kept the locket, and she now handed it to Joanna: it was engraved

'Eleanor Wiseman, May 14, 1641'. Nora also told Joanna that she knew Nelly's mother had a sister called Visscher. After this the clergyman Richard Hazell re-entered the tent and administered the last rites to the old gypsy.

Joanna walked back to Flaxley with Richard Hazell, and she told him about Nora's disclosures. He advised saying nothing to Nelly in case it wasn't true and unsettled her. Joanna also told him that Nora had mentioned the name 'Visscher' as being that of Nelly's mother's sister, but that she was sure it couldn't be the Isabella Visscher her brother James had married, because she had no sisters. In fact, one of the understandings of the marriage had been that she was an heiress and an only daughter.

A few days later, Mr Hazell called on Joanna and said that he'd been giving the matter some thought and felt the best course of action was for him to go to London and talk to James Boeve. Both he and Joanna wrote to James, he to ask for an interview, and Joanna to tell her brother that the vicar of Flaxley was coming to see him on important private affairs.

While this was going on, two other people were also trying to unravel the story of Eleanor Wiseman. One was John Langley who we had last met at William Boeve's deathbed; and the other was Mrs Anne Aylway who had approached Isabella at the soirée and asked after Eleanor her girlhood friend, Isabella's sister. In fact some time before William Boeve's demise, Mr Langley had called on Mrs Aylway in an endeavour to interest her in charitable works; as an example of a deserving case, he had by chance mentioned a gentlewoman called 'Eleanor Wiseman' who had fallen on hard times. Hearing her friend's name, Anne Aylway had implored the minister to take her to Eleanor – but when they got to the lodgings they were told she had left, and without giving a forwarding address.

Mr Langley knew there was a connection between the Visscher and Boeve families. When he attended William Boeve in his dying hours he attempted to ask him for more information on Eleanor Wiseman, but William became agitated, and bitterly regretting his attempt, Langley dropped the subject.

Meanwhile Mr Hazell kept his London appointment with James Boeve, and from him James learned that his wife Isabella had not been an only daughter. He then joined the search for Eleanor Wiseman: he went to see his father-in-law Samuel de Visscher who told him that yes, there had been an elder daughter, and she had been alive at the time of James's and Isabella's marriage, but that she had since died. James did not know of Mr Langley's fairly recent dealings with Eleanor Wiseman, and so he believed his father-in-law.

Mr Hazell therefore went back to Flaxley and told Joanna about James's findings; she was disappointed, and life went on as normal with Nelly knowing nothing of the matters which could concern her. However, one morning whilst cleaning her mistress's room, Nelly found the little gold locket inscribed 'Eleanor Wiseman' and, puzzled because it was her name, asked Joanna where it had come from. Joanna told her about Nora Cree's dying revelations and how steps had been taken to find Eleanor Wiseman, but to no avail.

Three years went by. Abraham Clarke continued to live and work away from Flaxley, and this was a relief to his mother who knew his feelings towards pretty Nelly. However, despite being in London society, Abraham showed no signs of marrying.

James Boeve went about his business. Then one morning as he walked past a bookshop which sold news-sheets he noticed a name on the top copy which stopped him dead: it was 'Eleanor Wiseman', and beneath was a solicitor's notice asking for anyone who knew of her to contact that solicitor's office. James bought the paper and hurried to the address given, and there he learned the following: the solicitor was acting on behalf of a deceased client, Mr George Wiseman, a childless widower; his only son had left him years earlier to be married, and not long afterwards had been killed at the Battle of Naseby. George Wiseman in his dying days had asked the solicitor to find out if his dead son's wife was still alive, and to locate her and the daughter he knew she had; the only information he could give to the solicitor was that she had been the daughter of a Dutch merchant named Samuel de Visscher.

James went home and confronted Isabella with the fact that he knew about her sister Eleanor, and she confessed that three years earlier Anne Aylway had informed her that Eleanor was living in London. James went to see Anne Aylway, and she told him all she knew: that Samuel de Visscher had married twice; that his first wife had borne him Eleanor, but had died soon afterwards; that he had married again and had two children, Isabella and her brother Sam; and that Eleanor as elder stepdaughter had felt unhappy and isolated at home. She also knew that the de Visschers were friendly with a family called Wiseman; George Wiseman, a handsome young soldier, visited often, and evidently Isabella had set her heart on marrying him. But to everyone's surprise he proposed to Eleanor instead, and she accepted him.

Anne Aylway bought a tiny gold locket for her as a wedding present.

Isabella was furious with Eleanor, and her father Samuel de Visscher sided with her and altered his will, disinheriting Eleanor and making Isabella and Sam his legatees.

After a brief spell of happiness, Eleanor was widowed when her husband was killed in the Civil War. He never saw his small daughter. Eleanor tried to make contact with her own family, but received little charity and eventually lost contact with them.

James Boeve returned from Anne Aylway and wrote all that he had learned to his sister Joanna. He ended by saying that although Eleanor Wiseman appeared to be dead, at least her daughter lived: she was of course Nelly, the maidservant, and the gold locket was proof of it; and so Joanna was able to say to Nelly: 'Dear child, you are no longer a penniless waif and a servant, but James Boeve's niece, and sole heiress to your grandfather Wiseman's fortune…'

Not long after this, Abraham returned home and married Nelly. However, that is not the end of the tale.

In the spring of the following year, 1665, plague broke out in London; this fact is backed up by a letter in the Flaxley Abbey archives, one which is quoted by Sybella Boevey as she continued the story of her ancestors. The letter is from Anne Aylway to her daughter Susan, and there is much in it about the ravages of the disease. For example, '…seventy or eighty thousand to fall in London in twelve weeks' time, and how many more yet we know not'.

Opposite: James Boeve

Flaxley Church and Abbey from Welshbury Hill

With plague rampant, people in London stayed indoors fearful to venture out, and this included Isabella Boeve. Anne herself had at first gone out on charitable works, but finding her efforts useless, she too stayed in. Then one day a beggar boy accustomed to calling at her house for kitchen scraps asked if she would visit the house where he and his grandfather lived, because a lady seamstress who lodged with them had been taken ill there. After ascertaining that the symptoms of this illness were not the same as those of the plague, Anne followed the boy; the house was within ten minutes' walking distance, and when they entered its front door, Anne found that the frail woman slumped upon the floor was Eleanor Wiseman. She had suffered a stroke.

Anne arranged to have her taken back to her own house where she was nursed back to health, although it was some time before Eleanor regained the power of speech. She was told about Nelly, but unfortunately because of the plague the two could not meet. Within a few weeks Eleanor suffered two further strokes which sadly led to her death.

Nelly and Abraham Clarke lived long and happily at Flaxley. Their joy was saddened, however, by the deaths of their three little children.

POSTSCRIPT At the time Sybella Mary Crawley Boevey wrote *The Gipsy's Fosterling* she noted that the names of Nelly and Abraham's little children could still be seen on a tombstone in Flaxley churchyard; but when I visited the churchyard I couldn't see the tomb, despite searching hard. However, it could be there.

Nearby Flaxley Abbey makes an impressive backdrop to the churchyard. The church itself is not the one of Nelly and Abraham's day; it was built in 1856 to a Gilbert Scott design. However, a few old memorials from the former church have been saved and are near the altar, and one is to Abraham Clark who died 4 December 1683 aged sixty-one; the text on it is a eulogy in Latin to his fairness, justice, loyalty, generosity and liberality. There is no sign either inside or outside the church of a memorial to Nelly. There is, however, a largish tomb on the south side of the church, and one can imagine that this is where Joanna Clarke might have laid the ten pounds which bought Nelly from the gypsies.

And concerning gypsies, in a strange tale of coincidences, here is a final one: when I talked to Sybella's great-great-great-niece Pattie about Sybella and her gypsy's fosterling story, Pattie told me that, oddly enough, that very week a group of gypsies had camped on Welshbury Hill, near the abbey and the very place where Joanna Clarke and Isabella Boeve met Nora Cree, and where Joanna had first seen Nelly. I was so struck by this eventuality that I decided to visit the gypsies, and the next day toiled up the hill to find them. At first I thought they'd gone, for even after climbing for some time there was no sign of them, and I began to waver because I wasn't even sure I was going in the right direction; then suddenly I saw a hobbled piebald horse, and above it, in a grassy clearing amongst the trees, a collection of gypsy waggons. Smoke was trailing from their chimney stove pots – and sitting on the very first waggon was a fair-haired child!

'New age gypsies' on Welshbury Hill

However, it wasn't the ghost of little Nelly; in fact it wasn't a little girl at all, but a boy called Jareth. His mother, Sian, was preparing food inside the green canvas cover of the waggon. They were part of a group of 'New Age' travellers living in old gypsy waggons and leading a gypsy existence.

Sian took me round and introduced me to everyone. They were friendly and some said they had gypsy blood in their family. I told them about Sybella's story and how Nora Cree had camped on the very same spot 300 years earlier. Sian said that they wouldn't move off for a week or two, and as they had an address at which they could pick up mail, I said I'd send them *The Gipsy's Fosterling*; I did, but I don't know what they made of it.

FRED STEPHENSON

꧁꧂

'I lead a selfish life, but I don't interfere with anyone' – and thus saying, Fred Stephenson lifted the hot lid of his iron stewpot with a forked twig and examined its contents. Satisfied, he replaced the lid and tucked the twig back into a link of the chain on which the pot dangled over an open fire. A few cooking utensils hung on an overhead bough, and a teapot and cups were spread on a nearby collapsible, red formica-topped table. The creamy heads from a stretch of hedge parsley rose behind the table and beyond them, reached by a slight dip, was a small ragged coppice.

Fred's cooking and dining area was in fact the inner cusp of a lay-by, a useful stopping place off the cross-roads of a 'B' road with a 'C' road. The lay-by was in the first section of the 'C' road, and Fred's cooking area was partially screened from passing motorists by his parked caravan and square, yellow ex-British Telecom van.

Fred is sixty-two. He is a man of many roads, but still has the strong lazy accent of Suffolk where he spent his boyhood. 'It annoys me, everyone thinks I come from Norfolk, they don't recognise a Suffolk accent and it's the twelfth biggest county in the country,' he grumbles good humouredly. He is a calm, good-tempered man, but there, as he says, 'The fire, me dogs and birds never argue with me.'

His birds live in the yellow van, which also pulls his little caravan. The inside of the van is fixed up with wooden cages, and in them are different sorts of canaries. For example there's a greenfinch mule, the result of his crossing a cock greenfinch with a Gloucester canary. He explained, 'Any finch which is crossed with a canary is a mule; so a goldfinch cock crossed with a hen canary is a goldfinch mule.' In other cages there are green lizards; also fife and border canaries.

'I've kept birds all me life. See that big ol' canary?' – he indicated a superior-looking specimen – 'You can hear it half a mile down the road. A lady taped all my birds once; she came at half-past three in the morning to do it. I was up ready for her. There's nothing better than to sit down in the morning, have a cup of tea and watch the birds.

'If they're pairing up they regurgitate and feed one another – it's a bonding sign; so that night I shine a torch in and move 'em into a nesting box. Couldn't do it in daylight, the stress would be too much.'

Fred breeds his birds for sale at travellers' fairs. 'Years ago you'd take a cock goldfinch from the wild and put it with a canary, but you're not allowed to trap them now. You used to

Opposite: Fred Stephenson

57

do it using either of two ways. One was with a riddle which you'd raise up by supporting it with a forked twig; this had a string on it. You'd sit and smoke a pipe, and wait for birds to come under the riddle after food you'd put there, then you'd pull the string and the riddle would come down over them.

'The other way was to boil up holver bark – you'd probably call it holly, we call it holver – boil it, then skim the grey gluey substance off the top of it three or four times and put a drop of linseed oil in that. You'd watch where the birds roosted, put it on, and in the morning they'd be waiting for you, their feet stuck.'

Fred spoke of seeing a little flock of goldfinches, eight or ten of them on some teasel on the morning of the October day I called on him. He's also seen 'fulfers' (fieldfare) and 'hances' (herons).

He is a tall, good-looking man with a tidy, greying beard, and his pipe is rarely out of his mouth. His uprightness hides the fact that he has a back injury: 'When I was in my thirties I was carrying corn, sixty tons a day, piecework. I was loading a forty-foot trailer with sacks, and each one weighed twenty-four stone, that's three hundredweight, and it did my back in. The shorter you are, the better you can carry that sort of weight – it's less of a strain.'

His father, Percy, was forty-nine when Fred was born, and the family had spent their days in Suffolk and Norfolk. They never travelled far because his father's health was poor, and how far they went was also dictated by how easily they could find grass for the horses. Fred had one brother, and the family travelled alone, never in a group. He told me their name was spelt 'the long way', and later I was to see it in the signature of Tom Stephenson on a beautifully painted waggon at Appleby Fair. Tom, now deceased, was Fred's second cousin and a noted waggon painter.

When he was with his family, Fred helped with the selling of horses, pegs and dogs. He said proudly: 'Every penny you took was yours, and we never had any bills. It's the same with me today, when I got a generator I paid for it there and then, and if I want anything, I make it.'

He started travelling on his own when he was seventeen. He had a mare and a waggon, and lived off money that he earned from casual farmwork. He'd used a horse up until fifteen years ago. 'Then the price of horses became ridiculous. They've levelled out now, but it's not practical to travel by horse waggon today. There aren't many village shops and you can't take horses into supermarket car parks. I wouldn't go back to it, and you've got to move with the times. Do you know why travellers have coloured horses?' he queried.

'No,' I admitted.

'To pull their caravans!' He beamed and puffed on his pipe. It wasn't the last of his quips.

Opposite: Fred with dogs and birds; (above) waggon painting by Tom Stephenson, Fred's second cousin

On the ground near the caravan door he keeps two wooden cages with runs made from old fireguards, the materials used in their construction salvaged from tips. One cage holds a ferret, a fluffy, yellow-coated little creature, the other his polecat, streaky-brown with white fur edging its ears and white patches on its face and beneath its chin. Nearby is their carrying box, also home-made. Fred maintains that the animals are happy enough in their cages because they like confined spaces – in the wild they live in holes. He once mated the ferret to the polecat (a female) and she produced three kits in the ensuing litter; two he'd sold in Norfolk, and one at Stow Horse Fair. Knowing their capacity for biting, I look at the ferret and polecat cautiously, and Fred admitted that he'd got ferret bites everywhere. Then he said: 'But the cougar's the most dangerous animal on earth' – then after a pause, 'No, come to think of it, my old woman was!' and beamed at me again.

Fred proudly displays the 'Althorp Estate' hacker

I've only seen him annoyed a few times. The first occasion was on a day when we were sitting on fold-up chairs by his campfire eating the stew he'd made and slices of bread fresh from the baker's in the local town. A passing car slowed down and then stopped, and the couple inside stared across the road at us. Fred was visibly upset: 'Annoys you when you get stared at, no manners. I wouldn't stare into their house. If you put a scarf on your head you could offer to tell their fortunes.' The couple eventually moved off and Fred put some small pieces of wood on the fire to liven it up sufficiently to boil the kettle for tea.

He cuts his wood with a hacker which came from the Althorp estate. It has 'Earl Spencer' and beneath that 'Woodman' stamped onto the blade. Fred says he bought it. He uses dead wood and keeps it dry by storing it under the caravan at night. As he was feeding the fire, Fred told me of a gypsy tradition: 'When you moved off a spot you'd leave enough wood for the next bloke so that he could make a cup of tea before he started scavenging for his own fuel. It's a custom long gone.'

I asked if there were other fireside traditions. 'It used to be correct if you were approaching someone sitting by the fire to call out first to let them know you were coming, you didn't just come out of the darkness on them. They would then say "Come on" or "Get off". Also you never used to see women sitting round the fire with men; they had their own fire. There's still one or two at Stow who leave the fire when the men come up. You see, there's men's talk and women's talk. In bender tents all the women are at one end.'

A second time I saw Fred ruffled was at Stow Fair. I was looking out for his yellow van in the row of traders which line a roadway outside the horse-selling field, but when I spotted it I held back because a man in a suit was talking to him. He was from the local council, and he was telling Fred, and the other livestock traders, that they weren't allowed to sell their

Waiting for customers at Stow Fair

birds or dogs at the fair. Fred, who'd already sold a puppy, complied – but as a result he quite lost the *bonhomie* of spirit that the show usually engenders in him, and muttered darkly about the Mayor of Casterbridge selling his *wife* at a fair. He'd heard this Hardy story on his radio and had been very taken with it.

Stow Horse Fair in the spring and autumn is the nearest and surest way I have of contacting Fred. He doesn't read or write, has no mobile phone and travels the year through, so communication at other times is difficult. When I saw him last he'd made fourteen moves in five months: he'd stayed at Benmore; Melrose; Fell End; Barnard's Castle; Appleby; somewhere in County Durham; Shipton; Consett; Pool (outside Otley); Green Hammerton; Sizewell; Northampton; and had then come back to Stow. The furthest north he goes is Dunnit Head. 'Travel's an education,' he once told me. 'I may be uneducated but I'm not ignorant. I broke the jaw of a man in a pub for calling me an ignorant didicoy… I had to go to court over it.'

Despite seeming to be perpetually on the move, Fred says that on average his yellow van only clocks up about six and a half thousand miles a year. 'That surprises people, but once I've settled in a place I don't go anywhere except to the nearest town, say, a mile away.'

I haven't mentioned much about Fred's dogs and I should, because they and his birds are his life. He hunts with them and breeds from them; he usually has four, and favours lurchers:

'You can get a lurcher by crossing a greyhound with a collie. You get speed from the greyhound and stamina and brain from the collie.' Then there are whippet crosses like Fred's dog Toby. He explains his pedigree thus: 'He's half whippet, quarter Bedlington Terrier and a quarter Bearded collie. I could have sold him for twelve hundred pounds but I wouldn't part with him.'

Some people buy lurchers from Fred for hare-coursing competitions. Fred explained coursing: 'A whole lot of men walk a field in a line, and one bloke will have two dogs on a slip-leash; the hare gets up, and she's always a hundred yards away before the dogs are released both at the same time. The dogs will have different coloured collars, say, one a red collar and the other a yellow. The winner is the one which turns the hare most times until she gets away or gets caught. Three hares are put up, and travelling boys will lay bets on the overall winner, that is, the best performance over the three hares; so the dog which catches two, wins. I think it's silly, meself – I like me sport on me own, going out on me own.'

During last summer one of Fred's dogs, Bella, was killed when she ran onto a railway line in pursuit of a rabbit and was struck by a train. Fred told me sadly about the accident: 'She was good, only young, I went and picked up her head and the other pieces and buried them. She'd been born on the side of the road and was used to catching rabbits and pheasants. She was a year and eleven months old when I buried her. That evening I got blind drunk.'

Fred's grief over losing Bella is partially assuaged by his puppy Little Bella, the offspring of Toby and Sheba (a blue Merle bitch). Fred had bought Sheba at Stow not long ago from Essie Taylor; Essie comes from Cannock and sells a lot of secondhand harness at the fair.

Fred has a set routine when he's buying a dog: 'The first thing I look at is its teeth – if a dog's, say, eight months old, its teeth will still be small. Then I look at its ears; when I felt

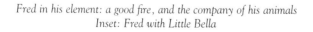

Fred in his element: a good fire, and the company of his animals
Inset: Fred with Little Bella

the ends of Sheba's ears they were rough, and that meant she was a good hunter as they'd been torn by blackthorn and brambles when she worked the hedges. I like a dog that can work a hedge, because I'd sooner eat a pheasant than a hare any day.'

He also explained to me his method of training a dog for life on the road: 'I give it a short name it'll know and answer to, and I teach it commands like "sit", "stay" and "stand". I teach it to hunt by following the older ones, and I get it to retrieve by stuffing a rabbit skin and throwing it like a ball.

'Once a fortnight I boil some young nettles for all the dogs and mix them up with their food. It cleans their systems. I keep 'em wormed, too. Years ago you used to be able to get some powder called "Recky" to do that; it looked like nutmeg. It's illegal now. Not long ago an old boy near Otley asked me to give him a rabbit head to worm his dog – could be the brains in it, I suppose.'

Fred feeds his ferret with rabbits the dogs catch, and of course the ferret is used to catch rabbits, too: 'I put the ferret down the rabbit hole, then put a net over the entrance. Sometimes I'll net six holes, but some I don't net because I like to give the dogs a run. The ferret drives the rabbits out into the net.'

Fred hunts the roadside hedges, but often has bigger grounds: 'There are three or four estates I can stay at, any time I like. I've no trouble with the country gentry – it's the ones which come out of towns to the country I can't get on with.'

He has his own rules on shooting: 'Never shoot anything which is harmless in life or useless in death. So you shoot a rat which is harmful, and a pheasant which is useful. Magpies are harmful, nothing preys on a magpie, but they takes eggs and young birds out of the nest, little harmless woodland birds.'

Years ago he used to hunt with a gin trap, although he knew they were illegal. When he was about twenty-one he caught his hand in such a trap and it severed a finger, but he didn't go to a doctor because he feared questions might be asked; he just wrapped a bandage round his injury and carried on. One day in a pub the landlady said to him, 'Your hand stinks – let me look at it.' He'd got gangrene, and the doctor who treated it told him that if he'd been older it would have killed him.

It was a sobering story, but Fred then brightened things up by showing me how to call a fox. He sucked the back of his hand making a squeaking sound, and told me that the fox would think the noise was a rabbit and come for it. It apparently works for weasels and stoats, too. He also demonstrated how to make a magpie answer with a three-quarter empty box of matches (Swan Vesta recommended) – rattle it three-and-a-half times, and the bird will answer the rattle. This particular training session finished with Fred asking: 'Why can't the viper wipe her nose? 'Cos the adder 'ad 'er 'anky!'

Catching pheasants is a task shared by Fred and the dogs. Toby is a past master at it, and given a moonlit night, so is Fred. He uses his catapult, and makes his own shot for it by melting lumps of lead into a little mould. 'The smaller the shot, the faster it travels,' he explains, adding: 'A pheasant will roost at seven in the evening, and by nine will have tucked its head under its wing; then it'll look like a dinner plate.' This is a fitting analogy, because Fred is something of an epicure about his food. For example on pheasants: 'I'll skin 'em, then pull the whole breast off and roast it; beautiful food with potatoes and parsnips. The rest of it goes to the dogs and the ferret.'

On rabbits: 'You need pork fat with rabbit because it's all lean meat. I fry young rabbits with onions or wild mushrooms.'

On mushrooms: 'A little drop of pork fat, and salt in the middle of each when you take 'em out of the pan. Puffballs are OK done in butter, and blueies – ones on blue stems – are nice. Shaggy inkcaps are eatable, but ordinary inkcaps make you feel ill if you've had a drink. There's only about eight poisonous fungi out of two hundred; basically anything with red spots, and anything "pixie-capped" is not good.'

And on rosehips: 'Boil 'em, take out the centres and drain the juice off, then add what's left to blackberries and crab-apples.' Fred is also partial to wild fennel which grows up north, and to horseradish which he digs up, scrapes, and then grates into vinegar, storing it in a

screw-top jar. When talking about food he says: 'I live on my name, so I don't nick out of fields, and I get water from springs or from petrol stations.'

Occasionally his refreshment comes from unexpected sources. At one of his stopping places a local teacher brought her class along to talk to him, and afterwards asked what he'd like by way of a thank-you. He'd replied: 'A big cake, a good ol' big 'un!' – and he'd got it.

Fred's life seems idyllic; he even enjoys winter time with the fire going and the frost around: 'If you have a good breakfast and keep your shoulders and feet dry, you won't come to much harm. An old-fashioned doctor told me that. Years ago we used to tie sugar-beet hessian sacks round our legs when we sat by the fire. Mother used to make aprons from 'em.'

He has few material treasured possessions: a little clay pipe which belonged to his grandmother with a venerable metal match-case, and the model of a gypsy waggon he made out of matchsticks. He's also happy enough with his little caravan, nut-brown inside and decorated with round transfers of wildlife scenes. He told me that his daughter (I know nothing of his family who seem not to travel with him) had put up the pictures one winter recently when he'd had a spell in hospital; he'd found them up when he came out. He'd gone there because he'd fallen whilst he was out rabbiting, and had smacked his head against a tree; a gamekeeper had found him, frozen solid, and he'd been in hospital with pneumonia for weeks. The gamekeeper kindly looked after his dogs and birds.

Fred knows that time is going on, that his back is injured and that he has arthritis. But he says: 'I don't like rules, and on gypsy sites there are rules and regulations. I've my tobacco and tea, and I live for the day – and each one's a bigger bonus as time goes by.'

JACK & GEVONER LOCKE

When this book was no more than an idea and I was pondering over an almost empty research file on the kitchen table, an odd thing happened: there was a knock at the door, and on the step stood a woman in a pink crocheted jumper and black skirt. She said, 'Will you buy something from a poor gypsy?' and started to dip her hand into a wide leather bag on her arm. I couldn't believe my eyes, for I could count on one hand the calls from gypsies I'd received over the years. I said, 'Come in, come in.' She looked at me warily, and I added hastily: 'I'd like to talk to you for a few minutes about some research I'm doing on gypsies, if I could please.'

She still looked suspicious, then said, 'My daughter's in the car, I'll just go and speak to her.' I left the door open, and she returned and came into the kitchen. I explained that I'd like to meet gypsies who would talk about life in days gone by. She said, 'Well, I'm no good – I'm too young.' She was probably in her forties, and told me her name was June Price. Then she said, 'If I tell you someone, will you buy something from me?'

'Yes', I said rashly.

'Gevoner Locke will talk to you.'

'Where is she?'

'Briton Ferry.'

'Where's that?'

'Between Port Talbot and Swansea.'

'What's her address?'

'I don't know – now you'll buy something from me?' and she produced a mat crocheted from string, not quite as big as a dinner plate in size. The price she asked made my eyes widen, and it rose when I discovered I had only one note in my purse, upon which she said quickly, 'I haven't got any change!' The note became hers – and in truth I am eternally gratefully to June Price, because I did go to see Gevoner Locke.

I turned up outside Gevoner's caravan one afternoon without having made an appointment, because not knowing exactly where she lived I had no way of contacting her beforehand. A smallish man with a moustache and wearing a neat, old-fashioned collar and tie, opened the caravan door to me. I explained I'd come to talk to Mrs Locke about days gone by, if she'd see me, and apologised for appearing out of the blue.

I was asked in and made welcome. It was Jack Locke, Gevoner's husband, who had

Opposite: Gevoner Locke

67

opened the door; Gevoner herself was sitting on a bed, because ill health prevents her moving far. She had lovely skin, tawny but pinkish on her cheeks; round her neck was a necklace hung with sovereigns and half sovereigns.

Jack told me that he was eighty-six and Gevoner eighty-three; their respective fathers were cousins so Gevoner's surname had never changed. I subsequently found out that the Lockes are respected aristocrats of their kind, and Jack and Gevoner's trailer certainly befits their status because the fireplace has a burnished silver surround, the mirrors are ornate and silvered, and the ceiling light-fittings are fancy glass. It is a magnificent vehicle, a 'Roma Special' made by a firm in Morecambe, according to Jack.

I remarked tentatively that 'Gevoner' was an unusual name, and she replied that she thought she'd been christened after Abergavenny, the town on the Welsh borders, although

her family had come from North Wales, from Anglesey. Her father's name was Charlie Vivian Locke, and he was a younger son of Noah and Delaia Locke. Her mother hadn't been a traveller, and she had met him when he was playing in a band at a dance. He was one of six brothers, all of whom played musical instruments; the Lockes have always been noted as musicians. When Gevoner told me this, I remembered the tales I'd heard of a 'Fiddler' Locke who played in the towns and pubs of Herefordshire years ago; I mentioned this, and Jack considered it must have been 'Winkles' Locke, the best of all gypsy fiddlers, but before his (Jack's) time. Gevoner said their own sons had inherited the musical trait.

The Lockes have three sons: Jack, Jimmy and Joe, and Jim showed early musical talent. When he was fourteen, his father had to lay tarmac in a yard where there was an old piano, and to clear it, the owner asked them to take the piano away. But Jim had said, 'Don't break

it up, let me have it, Dad!' So they took it back to some ground they were renting and covered it with a galvanised sheet. Not long afterwards Jack and Gevoner were coming back from the Gower, and when they were a hundred yards or so from home they heard a merry rendering on the piano of 'When You Are In Love' – and there was Jim sat at the keyboard. He'd repaired the instrument, and taught himself to play it!

I asked Gevoner how she and Jack came to marry, and she told me it had been in Anglesey. Her parents had stopped travelling when she was seven; they'd bought a house, but had kept their vardo beside it. Gevoner had gone to the local school until she was fifteen, and had loved it; then she went into service at a house in the seaside resort of Rhosneigr. During one of her yearly fortnight holidays at home Jack had come over to talk to her father, and they had married soon afterwards.

At first they had lived in a 9ft by 9ft (3m by 3m) 'kitchen' tent, square like a shed, and with a stove in it. They had travelled with it round North Wales. I asked Gevoner how she had adapted to travelling life, and she replied thus: 'Well, I was pally with Jack's sister, and I learnt hawkin' by going out with her and listening to what she had to say. I got used to the life quick, the making of paper flowers and pegs, and later I went to fairs with a caravan telling fortunes. My mother was a great fortune-teller, and I'd learned from her. You only have one in at a time, with two you get moithered.'

Gevoner and Jack Locke in their splendid caravan

DUKKERIN'

Dukkerin' (fortune telling) was, and still is, a way for gypsy women to earn money. Some gypsies say it is rubbish. Others, particularly women, defend it. They say that they learnt from their mothers and that they have been able to foresee events.

Eighty-six year-old Jack Locke recalls: 'Selling pegs at tuppence a dozen was just a front to keep the police away so that women could dukker. A lot of gypsy girls eloped because their fathers didn't like them having boyfriends. You see, they didn't like losing their daughters because they were breadwinners. They gave their fathers the money they earned dukkerin'.'

I asked if fortune-telling was true, and Gevoner didn't reply outright, but she told me of a prediction she had made which had become startlingly true; however, she asked me not to write about it. At this point Jack remarked that gypsy women hawkers got a 'slang' (the Romany term for a licence) for selling pegs and flowers, though usually it was just a front to keep the police away so they could dukker (tell fortunes).

I requested that he tell me about *his* early days. He'd been reading a newspaper whilst Gevoner and I had been talking, with half an ear to our conversation; now he came and sat beside me on a long, comfortable seat to the left of the caravan door.

'My father was James Locke, a horse dealer, and my mother was the daughter of Cornelius and Helen Shevlan. We used to travel through Shropshire and Cheshire with our relatives the Finneys and Boswells, in six caravans. We'd travel about twenty miles a day. Father had one caravan, but there were ten of us children and we couldn't all fit in, so most of us slept in a rod tent; we made this by cutting hazel sticks and sticking 'em into the ground, then we'd tie their edge and cover them with a blanket or sheet.

'The only schooling I had was six months in 1921 at Woolton near Liverpool.

'Our usual routine was that the men would drop the women off at a village so that they could sell their pegs and flowers. My mother sold lace: she'd buy it from Nottingham, they'd send it to her. The men would then go on to find a stopping place. If they turned off the main road they'd grab, say, five handfuls of grass and run over them with a wheel so they didn't blow away; that was called "patrins", and it told the women where the vardos had turned. Stopping places were usually a wide "flat", or verge, big enough to take all the caravans and twenty to fifty horses. The men would tether the horses – it was fairly quiet then, not a lot of cars about until after 1935 – and make a campfire. They'd get the wood by using a hooked pole to pull down dead branches from trees...'

Gevoner added: 'You'd use a "chump" – that's a small piece of dead hedge, say a foot across – for getting the fire going.'

Jack continued: 'The women would come back with their shopping, and we'd perhaps have jacket potatoes in the big fires. About ten o'clock we'd start to wait for the farmer to put his lights out so we knew he'd gone to bed. Then we'd make a gap in the hedge and put, say, fifteen of our horses into his field to graze; some were ones we'd bought for sale, some our working ones. This was known as "poovin' the grye".

'The idea was to get them out before the farmer got up the next morning, but sometimes he beat us to it and locked the gate. We might say that they'd got through the gap on their own, but sometimes it didn't work and he'd send for the police. When the police arrived he'd demand we paid him £2 or £3, and we had to hand it over. It was a lot of money and we didn't like parting with it, so sometimes one of our old ladies would start up a weird noise like this [Jack howled like a banshee] and she'd get out a crystal ball and look into it. She'd howl about three times, and a few others would go and look in the ball, then they'd look at the farmer, then at the ground, not saying anything. The farmer would get jittery and change colour, and at the same time a good, respectful gypsy would go up to him and say: "It's in your interest to give us this cash back – if you don't, you'll be looking back over your shoulder all your life."

'We did this once when we were stopping outside Chester; we'd been to the May races there. The policeman at that time had a bull-nosed Morris Cowley car; he was a ginger-haired fellow, and he said to the farmer: "Don't you listen to them, they're not worth a tinker's cuss!" But just as he said this, his car tyre went down – though I swear we hadn't touched it! Of course he thought we'd put the influence on the wheel…and the farmer gave us our money back.'

Jack laughed, and later I was to read in some books on gypsy history the theory that, generations ago, the Locke family had been known as Boswell; but because they encountered a spot of bother with farmers locking gates, they had changed their name, as gypsies were prone to do when avoiding the police. In the same way, at those times when it was convenient to do so, they'd revert to being Boswells! I can't vouch for the truth in this, however.

Jack, still thinking about farmers, told me of another old gypsy trick: 'It was to "drab the baulo" – that is, when the wife was hawkin' the farm, her man would poison a pig. Next day he'd go round and ask if there were any dead cows or calves – never mention the word "pig". If the farmer said there was a pig that had died, then he'd ask for it to skin so he could use the hide to make banjos. But because the poison he'd given it wasn't harmful to humans, when they got the pig back to camp they'd cook it for eating.'

In the late 1920s the Lockes, Finneys and Boswells went over to Southern Ireland. Jack remembers that time well: 'We found it was a very poor country. We tried to sell lino we'd taken over, but they wouldn't buy it. It wasn't very good material, we'd bought it at 10d a yard. They said they'd buy it, but would only pay 9d because it was "only old waxy", and they wanted more than a yard for that. So we gave up trying to sell it and we made stools out of orange boxes instead. There's three layers to an orange box and so we made three stools from one box. The boxes we got for 3d, 6d at most from fruit shops. We made the stool legs from willow, and put paper from old pattern books that we got from shops, glossy paper like wallpaper, on top of the stools. We also made three-legged tables from the orange boxes and we'd dye 'em with Bismark Brown stain. We used to be knockin' up these tables and stools till two o'clock in the morning!'

Storytelling was then momentarily suspended, for Kitty, the wife of Jack the eldest son, came into the caravan to see Gevoner and Jack; she lived on the unofficial gypsy site on adjacent common land. She hadn't been well, and Gevoner urged her to get a remedy from the chemist.

This was the first of several visits from the family. Son Jack, who looked remarkably like his father, also popped in, then a little later so did two of Gevoner's great-grandchildren, the grandchildren of son Jim and his wife Jean; they live in the caravan directly next door, and Jean and Jim live in the caravan opposite. Not long after that Jean herself came in. She said she was a 'Swede Nora' because she came from Herefordshire; so I said I must be too, and asked what they called Herefordshire men. 'The same,' she replied 'and if you're from Gloucestershire you're an "Old Spot" after the breed of pig.'

Jack looks after all the catering in the caravan because Gevoner finds it difficult to walk; now he was organising some food for everyone, and whilst he was doing so Jim, the middle

Gevoner's father, Charlie Locke

son, a tall, dark, handsome fellow, popped his head in the door. He grinned, and said to me: 'You're brave, eating with gypsies, mind he don't poison you!' Jim earns his living by doing landscape gardening, tree-cutting and building work; in fact, Gevoner and Jack told me proudly that he could turn his hand to anything. Jack added that gypsies didn't like their daughters to marry men who were gorgios (non-gypsies) because they weren't good at getting their own living, and found it difficult to adapt to gypsy life. They were also liable to have every penny robbed off them, and would always be outcasts.

I asked Jack and Gevoner if there were king and queen gypsies: they said there were not, and that any such belief was rubbish; however, some were looked up to, and in Jack's opinion this was '...generally the best fighter'. Even so, to have one gypsy over another was against their credo, whereby everyone was held to be equal. He went on: 'That's why gypsies are self-employed. "My boss": we hate those words! The only time gypsies usually had a boss over them was hop-picking, but we didn't go hop-picking because the money wasn't good and we could do better on our own initiative. A gypsy can do any sort of trade, and if he dresses up in a suit and polishes his shoes, people wouldn't know he was a gypsy.

'You'll never see a gypsy apprentice – we always learn by ourselves. About forty years ago I was at Priestweston in Shropshire and I saw a vibrator roll which weighed 800cwt and had an engine in it. We gypsies wondered what it was, because at that time no gypsy had ever laid tarmac. Then not long afterwards I was at Newborough in Anglesey and a lady had just had some tarmac laid – so I asked her how much the man had charged, but she wouldn't say. So I went to the local quarry, and they told me it was £2 a ton for hot stones and tar. I bought two small rakes from Woolworth's and decided to have a go for myself.

'On my first job I burnt the rake handles because they were wooden, and I also went off to dinner without covering the hot tar so when I came back it had gone hard as stone. I broke it up, put it on the drive and told the owner it was a base coat; then I got some more hot tarmac and finished the job. He said I'd done a good job. I'd never seen it done before, only seen it when it had been done.

'It was the same with sandblasting. In Hereford a few years ago I saw some men sandblasting houses. We gypsy boys didn't know what they were doing, so we watched 'em from a distance; we even followed them to Gyncoch and watched them sandblast a house there. They didn't know we were following or watching. When they'd finished we went to look at the equipment. There was a piece of bell-shaped steel with a hole in it and it hosed out compressed air and sand. I paid 10s for a small bag of sand, hired a compressor and we went to Morriston and got four sandblasting jobs.'

Gevoner said to me: 'I've helped him in everything he's done. For the past thirty years he's sold carpets and rugs.' Steering the conversation back to past times, I asked if they had any old photographs. They had none, except of themselves respectively as a young man and woman, and these two photos had been transferred onto china plates. Nevertheless, Jack could give more word pictures of his father's time:

'He taught me the "yaggers" (spectacles) trick. He'd buy several pairs of "gold"-framed spectacles from Woolworth's, 6d a pair. Then we'd go into a pub, and he'd ask if anyone had heard about the car accident earlier in the day. He'd get a pair of spectacles out of his pocket and say that he'd found them near the scene of the accident. He'd hint that they were no use to him, and that he'd probably sell them if anyone offered. As car owners in those days were generally rich, everyone listening assumed the glasses to have real gold rims, and 4s or 5s was soon offered, and accepted!'

Jack added: 'Do you know, you won't see gypsies wearing glasses if they're proper Romany; 80 per cent can't read or write so they don't get eye strain, and living outside helps. Green wood being burnt smokes and makes gorgios' eyes water, but not ours because we're used to it; and we needn't shield our eyes from the glare of snow. Gevoner can still thread a needle now, and we both read as if we were only aged twenty.'

Opposite: Jack Locke

JACK & GEVONER LOCKE

I couldn't dispute this, because Jack had indeed been reading his paper without the aid of spectacles. Whilst on the subject of eyesight I was reminded that gypsies had a reputation for not always seeing eye-to-eye, and asked Jack if he used to get involved in fights.

'Oh yes, you'd strip to the waist and tie a handkerchief round your waist. If you fought at night it was the custom to try and have a re-fight the next morning because it might have been drink giving your opponent Dutch courage to fight the night before. Sixty per cent of the time they wouldn't come out, especially if they'd lost the previous night.'

'What did you fight over?'

'Most fights were caused by robbing in horse dealing. All gypsies know a bit about horses, but some know a trick or two more than others. They'd sell you a bad feeder or one that was bobby-backed – that is, had hurt its back so that when it was pulling a caravan and coming down a bank it would be liable to fall. They'd run him up and down the road to show he wasn't lame, but you couldn't tell from that if his back was bad. Or they might sell a horse which turned out to be "nappy", that is, that wouldn't pull.

'Some old gypsies even managed to pass off as quiet, a horse that was prone to kick and jump. They'd tie some twist tobacco or some Battleaxe tobacco which came in a square plug, to the bit in the horse's mouth. He'd suck it, and it would make him dopey. The trick was not to leave it in too long, say only about an hour, because after that the horse's ears would droop.'

Gevoner: 'We used to buy horses at the fairs, and one pony we bought made a noise like a bull.'

Jack: 'He was asthmatical, we'd call him a "roller" or a "bull". In fact he fell down in the shafts and broke them. The fellow who'd sold him had given him linseed oil before the fair to loosen his pipes up, which was a dangerous thing to do. But we did tricks, too. If you were interested in buying a horse, say from a farmer, you'd sneak up to it when no one was watching, loosen its shoe and put a sharp bit of grit in, then tighten the shoe up; when it came out, it walked lame. We'd say it was lame in the shoulder and beat the price down. Of course, once we had it we'd loosen the shoe and take the grit out.

'At other times if a farmer said he wanted £30 for a horse we'd send a brother or son the next day to say such-and-such was wrong with it; then the following day we'd send someone else with another reason why the horse wasn't worth £30. Eventually the farmer would "go sick" – that is, he'd drop his price.'

Gevoner told Jack to tell me about the white horse, and he duly obliged. This had happened when they were in Ireland, because in addition to making furniture from orange boxes, they did some horse-trading. Unfortunately, they – that is, Jack and his brother Big Tommy – were taken in at a Belfast auction by a fellow gypsy. He'd rubbed a white horse's shoulder with a brick so that it looked as if it had been rubbed by a collar, and had then sold it to them. But later they found that it wouldn't pull, it wasn't a working horse. Jack explained how he tried to remedy the situation:

'I got some crystal potash to dry up the rub mark, but when I put it on the mark, dabbing it on with an old stocking, the patch of hair there turned dark purple and the skin beneath the same. I had to do something quickly, and I said to Tommy, "We'll make it a piebald" – and added more patches of dark browny-purple, a bit here and a bit there.

'A milkman passed our place every day and one day he said to my brother, "How much the ballee [piebald], Big Tommy?" So we sold it to him, and of course after a month the dark patches began to fade. He said to me, "That horse Big Tommy sold to me, he's losing his coat!" I said, "Oh, he's just changing it, horses do in spring. In fact they've even been known to lose their colour patches altogether!"'

Before I parted from Gevoner and Jack, Gevoner showed me a birthday card she'd had from her family; it was one she treasured, for it had a beautiful verse inside, about mothers. She also told me about their grandchildren and great-grandchildren, and recent family weddings. It is obvious that Jack and Gevoner live very much for today. However, there is a part of Gevoner's past that she did mention proudly: 'They put the red carpet out for my Aunt Izzie when she died; she'd danced in the streets of Paris, and her portrait's in the Academy in London.' When I asked her to tell me more, she told me to refer to a book called *My Gypsy Days* by Dora Yates: 'She wrote about us Lockes.' I did. I also read several other books and articles, and by piecing them all together, and after further conversations with Gevoner, I found out the extraordinary story of her Aunt Izzie. It should have a chapter to itself.

Some gypsy cures

Jack Locke's cure for backache or kidney trouble: 'Boil green celery tops plus pearl barley seed and parsley. Sieve and drink the liquid because it will wash out and coat the kidneys.'

A Hampshire remedy for curing warts: Impale a fat slug on a thorn on a branch of blackthorn, and as the slug shrivels away so will the wart…

… and for curing diarrhoea, eat the young, tender tips of a blackberry bush.

ESMERELDA LOCKE

Gevoner's Aunt Izzie, Esmeralda Locke, was born at Worfield in Shropshire in 1854, and she was to become a legend in her own lifetime, cliché though this may sound. Her dear friend of later years, Dora Yates, a scholar on gypsy matters, described her as having 'superb carriage' and possessing a 'beautiful, rich voice'. She also saw Esmeralda in many moods, described as 'courageous', 'imperious', 'passionate', 'violent-tempered', 'tender…' Esmeralda was the third child of Noah Locke and Dilaia Jones. She was christened at Worfield Church on 21 July 1854, and one of her godparents was Mr Samuel James, a friend of the local vicar the Reverend Broadbent (in fact Mr James went on to become a reverend himself).

At the time of Esmeralda's birth the Smith family was amongst those which held premier status in nearby Bridgnorth. John Jacob Smith was town clerk, and had taken over the post from his father before him. John Jacob had a son, Hubert, born in 1822. In his boyhood Hubert was interested in gypsies, and when he grew up he was accepted by them as a 'rai', a 'gentleman scholar'. He was a man of his time, interested in many subjects, and also in trekking and mountaineering.

Hubert was friendly with the Locke family, and in 1870 asked Noah and Dilaia if he could take their two eldest sons, Noah and Zachariah, on a camping trek in Norway: after all, what better members of a team than a pair who were used to walking, putting up tents and making campfires? The fourth member of the expedition was to be a friend of Hubert's. However, at the last moment this friend dropped out, so Hubert went to the Lockes to talk about this development, and it was arranged that Esmeralda, then aged sixteen, would make up the party to four. Her role would be to cook and to look after Hubert's tent. Hubert paid for new boots for his companions, and they set off by train and boat for Norway.

Hubert maintained the role of 'master' or 'employer'. They trekked by day, and in the evening Zachariah played his violin, Noah and Esmeralda tambourines, and Hubert a guitar; Esmeralda also sang. In fact, Hubert had composed a song called 'The Gipsies' Norwegian Song'. The brothers slept in one tent, and Hubert and Esmeralda in another with a divider between them.

Later, Hubert was to publish a book called *Tent Life with English Gypsies in Norway*, based on the diary he kept of this 1870 trek and a similar one the following year. It appears that the proper relationship of employer/adviser to Esmeralda was maintained, but Hubert did make some rather warm references to her in his diary – for example, on how well a skirt

Opposite: Esmerelda with her dog

and bodice fitted her, and that despite it not concealing her legs, 'she had no reason to be ashamed of her foot and ankle'. Indeed, by all accounts Esmeralda was by that time extremely attractive: tall, raven-haired, vibrant and with glorious eyes. Hubert also recorded Esmeralda picking flowers for his buttonhole and telling his fortune; and on one occasion he related how the two brothers had gone on ahead, and when the four had met up, the brothers had pretended in jest that they were meeting for the first time as strangers, and 'mistook' Esmeralda and Hubert as husband and wife.

Perhaps all this put the idea into Hubert's head – although again, maybe he didn't need much persuading – because when they got back to Shropshire he told Esmeralda's parents that he'd like to marry her. However, as she was only just sixteen, no date was set.

In 1873, Hubert became town clerk of Bridgnorth; Esmeralda was then aged nineteen. That year Hubert and the three went on another camping trip. The following year Hubert took Esmeralda to Christiania so that friends of his might teach her to read and write, and to understand music and different languages. Finally, on 11 July 1874, they were married; he was then fifty-two, and she was twenty. The following announcement appeared in *The Times*: 'Adrey Vallo Phillissin, Norway, the Rye, Hubert Smith, Esq., romando to Tarno Esmeralda Locke, who pookers covah Lava to saw Romany Palors.' Translated, this reads: 'At the Valley Herregard, Norway, the gypsy gentleman Hubert Smith married to the young Esmeralda Locke who tells this to all Romany brothers.'

When the couple came back to Bridgnorth they lived at a house called The Mundens; but Esmeralda's niece, Gevoner Locke, had told me that she wouldn't live in the house, but had a round tent in the grounds with a carpet in it. And so this seemed to be, because other people variously mention the fact, and an account written in the early 1960s by Mr Morley Tonkin, owner of *Shropshire Magazine*, relates that to please Esmeralda, Hubert had their bedroom windows taken out so that she wouldn't feel too confined! From the beginning it was evident that this was not a marriage made in heaven: Esmeralda had a quick, violent temper, and according to Mr Tonkin's account, locals spoke of her smashing crockery, windows and furniture.

Then at Christmas in the year of their marriage, Hubert invited a young man called Francis Hindes Groome to stay with them; Mr Groome had written to Hubert congratulating him on the publication of his *Tent Life with English Gypsies in Norway*. He came from an extremely respectable background, his father being Archdeacon of Suffolk. He was twenty-

three and a quiet, shy fellow with a love of folklore and an interest in gypsy life. He was certainly no swaggering Romeo, but the effect he had on Esmeralda was profound. In later years she told Dora Yates 'by God's truth, my Sister, when I saw that Rai and heard his voice it pierced my very heart, and I knew then that was my man. I loved him and he me, and when a Gypsy once kons [loves] like that, tuti jins [thou knowest], she koms for ever… From that day to this, even if he did treat me badly (though I treated him a lot worse!) I worshipped him, mira Pen!'

Soon after Francis's departure, Esmeralda told Hubert that she wanted to make a visit to her family at Newport – but Hubert discovered that she had in fact stayed with Groome in a hotel in Cardiff! When she returned home they had a furious row, and Esmeralda – in her words – 'felled' Hubert 'like an ox' with a blow from a pair of silver candlesticks. She even added, '…and that was good'. Hubert tried to get Esmeralda's parents to reason with her, because infidelity in marriage was against the Romany code (in fact in later years Ithal Lee, an uncle to Gevoner Locke, threatened to spit in Esmeralda's eye if they met up at the same function!). But it was all to no avail, and soon after her

return she went off to Bristol and stayed in a hotel there with Groome. Within a year of their marriage date Hubert started divorce proceedings.

Meanwhile Esmeralda and Francis Hindes Groome travelled across to the Continent. They had very little money, but Esmeralda worked in cafés, singing and dancing, and in this manner they went from Germany to France and Hungary, before eventually returning to England. A month before their return

Esmeralda had sent a contrite, begging letter to Hubert – though in a truly Thomas Hardy-style twist of fate he didn't receive it for several weeks, as he was away from Bridgnorth. When he did, he hurried to Edinburgh where Esmeralda and Groome had taken lodgings on their return. Esmeralda, seemingly full of remorse, agreed to return to Bridgnorth with Hubert, and spent the night in a hotel with him as their train did not go until the morning. However, in the hotel the next morning she told him she feared Groome would commit suicide, and said she wanted to go and say goodbye to him. Hubert let her, and she didn't come back. The divorce therefore went ahead, and on 20 November 1876 Francis Hindes Groome and Esmeralda were married.

Groome wrote books on gypsy life, and an article on gypsies for the *Encyclopaedia Britannica*. Theodore Watts-Dunton, a writer and gypsy enthusiast, introduced the couple to Bohemian society in London, and Dante Gabriel Rossetti included Esmeralda in some of his paintings.

Despite Esmeralda's divorce, her family gradually accepted her back, and she used to return to them for holidays. Francis got work as a proof-reader, and in 1885 became an editor of *Chamber's Encyclopaedia*. But his life of quiet studiousness was anathema to Esmeralda's temperament and increasingly they would fall out, and Esmeralda would leave him and go back to her family. Finally the situation deteriorated to such a degree that Francis, ill and fraught, wrote to Izzie in December 1898: 'I never wish you anything but good, Izzie, but we must never meet again on this side of the grave. Perhaps on the other side we shall.'

He died four years later; in his will his family were obliged to provide Esmeralda with an annuity for the rest of her days. Those she spent travelling with her family or by herself. She was well known in society circles, and would talk to journalists about gypsy life.

Hubert Smith eventually remarried and lived away from Shropshire. He died in 1911 and was brought back to be buried at Bridgnorth.

Esmeralda remained handsome and very upright into old age. She eventually settled in a caravan at Prestatyn in North Wales. Then in February 1939, at the age of eighty-five, she was going to collect her pension when she was knocked down by a bus. She was taken to the Royal Alexandra Hospital at Rhyl, where according to her friend, Dora Yates, she put up a gallant fight for life, and 'her proud spirit exerted itself over staff, patients and visitors'. Nevertheless she died on 4 April.

Esmeralda had expressed her desire to be buried not with gypsy ceremony, but as her husband Francis would have wished, with ordinary church rites. It was evident that she had loved him until the day she died. Her funeral therefore took place at St Thomas's Church, and Gevoner Locke told me that: 'They put a red carpet down from the hearse to the church, like for a Queen.'

Opposite: Esmerelda in Hubert's garden at Bridgnorth

FOOD NOTES

Les Elliott had a trout in a plastic jug full of water; this rested on an outside ledge of his open-lot. He was parked up for Stow Fair, and joked to me that he couldn't say where the trout had come from. At this point Edna, his wife, arrived back from town with a pram-load of shopping. She inspected the jug and said she didn't like trout herself, too slimy, but she'd cook it for Les nice and slowly with a knob of butter and pepper and salt.

I'd met Les and Edna several times before. They are East Midland gypsies and usually come to the Cotswolds for Stow Fair. I didn't press Les on the origins of the fish, but asked if he would be so kind as to tell me a bit about the food gypsies lived on in the days when most travelled full time. Les and Edna do still travel, but only from spring until autumn owing to Les's ill-health; they spend the winter in a house. Les replied to my query: 'It's the woman's duty to feed the family. She uses the money she gets from making and selling pegs and flowers and from telling fortunes. Occasionally she'll beg too, and barter, offering perhaps a yard of lace for some eggs. A lot of people used to feel sorry for a gypsy woman if she had a child with her, especially a baby slung on her back.

'The men would provide rabbit, hedgehog, hens, pigeons and fish. They'd take a chicken from a farm – not all the hens, just one to eat – and a cow cabbage, that's the big sort of cabbage grown for cattle fodder. They'd take a swede too, and some potatoes and peas. Swedes and taters make the best meal anyone can have, boiled and then fried next day with uncured bacon. If a man worked for a farmer he'd have his wage so much in money and perhaps the rest in bacon, and give a slice to the other gypsies if they hadn't any food. We helped one another to survive.'

I asked about methods of cooking, and Les replied: 'Shove a stick through to roast rabbit or birds, and the same for a breast of lamb.' But Edna said: 'I don't like a spit because it smokes. I like to roast in a pot over the fire. I can make anything on an open fire… shepherd's pie… anything. Although I can cook nice in an electric oven at the house in winter, outside it does it better!

'Even when we've got the electric oven, Les won't eat meat roasted in it, only done on top in a pot like on an open fire. I roast with cooking oil, put plenty into a pot over the fire and just leave it, let it go. When the fat's boiling I pull the pot to the side of the fire a bit so the middle does first, then put it back near the centre of the heat to make it brown, and really full on to get the crackling.

Opposite: Edna Elliott in her colourful 'summer residence'

'I boil me own ham, too. I don't like anything already prepared or cooked because then I wonder *how* it's been cooked; if I've done it myself I know it's nice and clean.'

I asked Edna what food she liked best. 'A lovely mushy pea soup is one of my favourites. I make it with a nice piece of brisket and gammon put in the pot and boiled till done but not dropped off the bone. Then I get them out and put in swede, onions, celery tops, leeks, dried lentils and carrots. I don't put in salt because the bacon is salt, and you can always put salt in when you eat it. When the veg is nearly done you drain all the water out and put in mushy peas. Makes a good, thick soup.

'I'd rather have rabbit pie than roast rabbit. Boil it so the meat comes off all the bones – there's a lot of small bones, too many in a rabbit – then cook the meat in a pie.'

'Did your mum teach you to cook?'

'No, I learnt meself. She wasn't a good cook, would do meals but not cakes or anything. To tell the truth, Mum and Dad used to drink a lot. I was the only daughter, and I had eight brothers, and I used to wash and cook for them, and for Mum and Dad. I used to mother 'em. I'd go round the hedges looking for blackberries and plums to make into pies and mess about with. In the horse-drawn waggon we had a little stove and I just tried to do things and they turned out all right.'

'Did you make jam and chutneys?'

'No, it's not something we do.'

Edna then admitted that she liked to cook with fresh produce: 'I go out for it every day. Also I'm at odds with Les when it comes to cakes and bread. He likes cakes after they've been kept, and bread when it's hard; but I always want to throw stale bread out.'

Another of Les's dislikes is shop-bought cake – he prefers ones made by Edna, particularly her 'gypsy cakes'. When I visited their house in late autumn Edna was about to make some. However, before doing so, she had to make four large apple pies for a social evening at their church. She and Les are Christians with a simple, strong faith. As she prepared the pastry for the pies she said: 'I like to use me hands – don't like electric mixers. We were given the apples, I wouldn't use that pie filling you buy in cans.'

Whilst the pies were baking, Edna washed up the utensils in a steel bowl: 'Les would go mad if I washed them in the sink, and no one ever washes their *hands* in the sink, but always in the bathroom or wash-basin in the downstairs cloakroom. I always wash things up after I've used them, so the only washing-up after a meal is the cooking pots and plates and cutlery.'

That done, Edna showed me a collection of iron pots in her cupboard; they double for the electric cooker and for the open fire when they're travelling in summer. She prefers

Les' favourite: 'gypsy cakes'

them to lightweight pots and pans. Another 'must' with Edna is to have four little pots each with a different food in: 'I like cabbage in one and greens in another, and I wash 'em as I go along. Years ago you used to have only one big pot on the grid over the fire because it cut down on the amount you had to carry around.'

Then she began to sort out the ingredients for the 'gypsy cakes': 'You need 12oz of flour which will make seven or eight cakes.' The flour went into a bowl. 'Next, whisk three eggs with a drop of water and a bit of salt in a jug,' which she did with a hand whisk. 'To the flour add roughly 2oz of lard and mix it in with your fingers, then 2oz of marge the same, so it ends up like breadcrumbs.

'Now you add currants or mixed fruit, as much as you like, I like a load of fruit. And finally add the eggs. You don't want the mixture too wet and sticky because you're going to pat the cakes out like a dumpling and flatten 'em, so if necessary add a bit more flour.'

Edna wiped her hands and took a flat, circular, cast-iron pan with a hooped handle out of the cupboard. She put it onto a ring to warm at 'middle' heat on her cooker; I noted that she didn't grease it. 'When I'm making these cakes over a stick fire I do it over dying embers and then they don't end up being done on the outside and not on the inside!'

Taking a handful of her mixture, Edna flattened and patted it until it looked like a small, fat pancake, slightly curving its outer edges so it wouldn't stick to its neighbour; she put it

Edna preparing gypsy cakes on her griddle

in the pan, and quickly did half a dozen more in similar fashion. When they were all in the iron pan, she put a frying-pan lid over them: 'You have to have a lid to keep the steam in because you can't keep 'em warm to cook otherwise, and they'd go flat and hard.'

As soon as they started to brown she turned them over, and kept turning until the knife she pushed in as a tester came out clean and unsticky and she was satisfied that they were done. She handed me one to taste. It was very good, and the mixed fruit definitely added piquancy. Les came in and sniffed the air appreciatively. He gave me his own brief recipe for the cakes, which was one egg, a pinch of salt and pepper, half a cup of lard, and as much flour as was necessary – and everything done with his fingers, even the egg whisking.

Hedgehog

A nineteenth-century gentleman passed through a gypsy encampment and was so struck by the cooking methods he observed being employed by and over various fires, that he wrote of it in his diary. He described having seen one gypsy eating a pudding out of 'No less than a "Jim Crow" hat', and… 'An old gentleman at another fire was "cooking his joint" so he said: but a strange joint it seemed to me. The smell was overpowering, and I could not make out what it was until I discovered it was hedgehog. The animal was skinned, cut in two, a stick pushed through like a skewer, and one end stuck in the ground in such a manner as to suspend the hedgehog over the fire. When it was cooked, each person pulled a limb off, and apparently devoured it with relish.'

If Jack and Gevoner Locke had been present at that roasting they would certainly have relished the 'joint' too. When I talked to them in their living trailer at Briton Ferry, they'd both agreed: 'We can't describe the taste of hedgehog – we call them Hotchi-witchi – it's like nothing else.' Gevoner said she could have eaten a whole one, there and then.

Jack said: 'You track 'em in winter because in summer they're too thin. I'll tell you how, and it's difficult because he only goes once down the track to where he's going to hibernate. At the end of September when the leaves are falling he drops his prickles down and drags himself along until he gets a heap of leaves and dried grass around him. Then, usually on the opposite side to where the wind is, the warm side of a hedge, he'll scrat a hole nine or ten inches deep, then drop the leaves, and you can't see him because he's covered in them and the dried grass.

'To track him, you look at which way the wind has blown a few things, then look to see if the undergrowth has been pulled the other way – it is difficult to see because, as I said, he only goes once down that track – and it's not a bald track like that made by a rat or a rabbit, and you've got to be clever to find it.

'Once you've found a hedgehog you carry it up under your arm and kill it. Get a rough knife which you've sharpened on a whetstone, hold him by one leg and scrape about 80 per cent of the bristle off. The stubble still left on you'd burn off over a fire, and when you're doing this he swells up. Then you cut him open nose to tail and take the entrails out. Give him a good wash and put him into salted water. The following day boil or roast him – but whichever way you cook him, eat with a bit of vinegar.'

Eli Frankham of Cambridgeshire gives some more hedgehog facts: 'People say that gypsies cook them in clay, but that's wrong. We don't cook anything with entrails inside.

'It's a meat stronger than pork or pheasant, it's like high game and there's not a lot of meat once the fat's melted. With any other meat you cook, the fat comes to the top with jelly underneath, but not with hedgehog oil. You can pour hedgehog fat into a bottle and it never settles. Old gypsies used to sit and clean harness with it, it strikes away dampness, strikes it away from the horse.'

The fish the herring has a fingerprint on either side of its head.

You mustn't eat red meat when people die.

GYPSIOLOGISTS

In 1888 two men of different backgrounds decided to do something about their mutual fascination for gypsies. They were American philologist and ethnologist Charles Godfrey Leland and a Scots historian named David MacRitchie, and they started the Gypsy Lore Society. Its aim was to 'investigate the gypsy question in as thorough and as many-sided a manner as possible'. They hoped to do this through a quarterly journal which would contain articles on gypsy customs, folklore and so on; its co-editor with MacRitchie was Esmeralda Locke's second husband Francis Hindes Groome. The society flourished for five years, then finally foundered through lack of money.

It was revived in 1907 when MacRitchie and a founder member John Sampson, librarian of University College, Liverpool, enlisted the help of a well-to-do Liverpool sugar refiner named Robert Andrew Scott Macfie. Despite his many business commitments, Macfie was a man who found time for artistic and scholarly pursuits, and the ensuing years were to prove his value to the society and his popularity amongst gypsies.

The 1907 revival coincided with the beginning of another society inspired by 'the open road': the Caravan Club, set up to cater for a new cult called caravanning. This was not the type of caravanning employed by showmen and gypsies, and which a magazine of the time described as being of 'a low tone', but caravanning for leisure. Such a caravanner (according to the same magazine) would have books, a bed and a chair with a roof over all, and 'would drift through the smiles and tears of sun and cloud and the beautiful sympathetic responses the earth makes to both'.

THE ART OF CARAVANNING

BY HUGH ALDERSEY

It was a far cry from the aims of the eager, earnest gypsiologists of the Gypsy Lore Society intent on collecting gypsy genealogies, stories, music and so on. However, many did spend their holidays travelling in gypsy vardos either owned by themselves, or hired. For example William Ferguson, whose home was at Tytherington, near Macclesfield, travelled with his brother in their own vardo. They often took a gypsy called Oliver Lee with them, not the least because he could make 'very comfortable' the gypsy tent they carried.

A publisher's invoice to Gypsy Lore Society member Herbert Malleson regarding copies of a book he had written about gypsy Napoleon Boswell

T.W. Thompson, a keen collector of gypsy folk tales, once wrote to a friend: 'I had a glorious time when I was collecting the material for my paper [for the Journal], making the acquaintance of a good half of the Norfolk and North Country Gypsies.' He travelled in a 'Romanichal's vardo' one August with Scott Macfie and fellow gypsiologist Eric Winstedt; and on another occasion he and several friends hired Esmeralda Locke's waggon for their gypsy tour.

A rather unlikely owner and user of her own gypsy vardo was Lady Arthur Grosvenor, of Broxton Lower Hall near Chester; she was to become president of the Gypsy Lore Society in the year 1913–14. A 1907 newspaper cutting describes her as 'petite and dainty'; her husband was uncle to the then Duke of Westminster. She spent months at a time travelling with her gypsy caravan; the brown vehicle is said to have been hung with baskets for sale and the cages for her two birds, and beneath it were slung frying pan, kettle and saucepan. Lady Grosvenor adopted the name 'Syeira Lee' for travelling, and wore clothes appropriate for her gypsy life – on one occasion she is reported to have been seen wearing a 'flaming red skirt, blue jersey, slouched straw hat and immense earrings'.

She was friendly with the Locke family, and when Esmeralda stayed near Broxton Lower Hall, she would call weekly to teach Lady Grosvenor Romani; indeed she proved an amusing and able teacher. The two became great friends and Esmeralda often went caravanning with her. Gevoner Locke told me that Lady Grosvenor used to travel with her father and mother, and that her father Charlie advised her on what horses to buy to pull her vardo; he also trained them for her to do shaft-work. Jack said, 'She "pooved the grye" too!' (slipped her horses into a farmer's field without permission at night, a gypsy trick). Gevoner added that she was too young to remember her much – though she knew that once Lady Grosvenor had put a scarf

This photograph taken at Brough Hill Fair, near Warcop, Westmorland, on 1 October 1911, shows (from left to right) gypsiologists Scott Macfie, Jas Ferguson, Rev George Hall and William Ferguson. Next to the cooking pot is gypsy Oliver Lee, who, like his younger brother, Ithall, befriended many 'Romani Rais' (gypsy scholars)

LADY ARTHUR GROSVENOR'S GIPSY CARAVAN.

Lady Arthur Grosvenor has a passion for caravan life. She spends a considerable part of each summer in wandering about the country lanes in her gipsy home. At present she is enjoying one of these unconventional tours in the caravan shown above. Inset is Lady Arthur Grosvenor.—(Lafayette.)

The Daily Mirror *of 10 June, 1907 reported Lady Grosvenor's caravanning trip*

over her head and tried to sell pegs at her own back door, but her servants sent her packing!

Lady Grosvenor travelled mainly around Cheshire, though she did make longer journeys to Brough and Appleby Fairs in Cumbria. She sometimes went even further north: for example on one occasion she wrote to her friend and fellow Gypsy Lore Society member the Reverend H. Malleson from Lochmore in Lairg; she described the weather and travelling conditions, which had been good for her journey except for one stretch:

'The only bad bit we had is about 32 miles from Lair to here. I met one of the Herons from Hull near Stirling, he had been to John O'Groats, and Mannie Buckland near Tain, they had been there too. The farmers, the other side of Stirling were awful, cld'nt get ice for ages, had to do 20 + 22 miles before being able to stop, but as soon as we got beyond Dunkeld they were all right.

'We did the last 15 miles by night, as the heat + horse flies on Tuesday were more than we cld stand again so we rested the horses, till 10 at night & then came on by the light of a full moon and at 1-20 it was quite light again, I cld see the time by my watch all night...'

My favourite gypsiologist from the pre-World War I years was Alice Gillington. I am afraid I say this only on the strength of having read some of her letters, but they are so full of character! She lived the year through in two caravans with her brother, and they travelled with the vans, one yellow, the other brown, around Hampshire; her letters are addressed as from: 'The Yellow & Brown Caravans, Thorney Hill' or 'Bitterne' or 'Fawley', or whatever part of the county they had stopped in.

Alice became godmother to various gypsy babies, wrote stories about Hampshire gypsies, and collected gypsy music and folksongs. She also spent some time teaching gypsy dances in local schools; these were out of her book *Songs of the Open Road*, and she hoped that they would be seen as useful alternatives to Morris dancing. Her nomadic life wasn't without frustrations, however, and in August 1911 she wrote:

'I find that no Gorgios have the very faintest idea what caravan life is like! It *can't* be mixed up with gorgio ways and habits, and this they don't (or won't) understand!… The afternoon caller is, with the exception of chickens and wasps, far and away the worst thing the caravan dweller has to put up with. It allows no rest. Afternoon calls don't *go along* with cleaning knives in a turf bank and washing clothes!…

'I expect I worried my own gypsies sometimes, when I was a house dweller.'

Late September of that year was cold, wet and windy. Their caravans got bogged down and her brother caught a chill. However, by early October he was well enough to enjoy Alice's caravan cooking: apparently on the 6th she served rabbit pie, potatoes cooked the Irish way, sago pudding, stewed quince, and apple and orange jelly. She also found time that day to complete a list of the mourners who had attended a local gypsy funeral and sent it off to Mr Macfie, although she didn't know if he would include it in the Gypsy Lore Society journal. Indeed Alice, like most writers, sometimes had difficulty in getting her work published. Once, when her publishers seemed to be getting cold feet over accepting a manuscript, she asked her fellow gypsiologists to create a demand for her work by writing to them asking for her last book. I wonder what she'd think if she could see that one of her books is currently being advertised in a secondhand bookseller's catalogue at £60!

In 1911 the Gypsy Lore Society found that it was no longer the only organisation for gypsiologists, because the Gypsy and Folklore Club opened its premises at 5, Hand Court, Bedford Row, London. It boasted of rooms decorated in 'the most approved Gypsy style', and of a library of gypsy and folklore books; it proposed to give concerts at which gypsy artists would appear, and to have exhibitions of gypsy craftwork; and it, too, had a monthly journal, and also notepaper headed with a hedgehog logo.

At first, Gypsy Lore Society members were well disposed towards the new society. Robert Macfie offered good advice to its founder, William Townley Searle, several members submitted articles for its journal, and the artist Augustus John became its president. However, soon there were rumblings amongst the Gypsy Lore Society stalwarts against Searle and his club; they weren't happy about the treatment given to their articles, and Searle's publicity gimmicks were not to their taste. Worse, he appeared to be deliberately deceiving people. For example, a gypsy appearing at one of his suppers as Jasper Petulengro was, according to a Gypsy Lore Society member, in fact Sampson Boswell who lived at Westbourn Park! The same member noted that on another occasion he presented 'third-rate Russian actors & English gâge' as the 'genuine article'.

In 1913 Augustus John became so angry with Searle that he went to Hand Court and broke all the glass he could get at with a stick. Searle retaliated by pinning up a notice saying:

'These windows were broken by the celebrated impressionist artist, Augustus John, in his eagerness to enter the club.'

Scott Macfie, at this time the driving force behind the Gypsy Lore Society, had serious misgivings about the Gypsy and Folklore Club and expressed his disapproval of it. Townley Searle began a libel action against him, and Macfie required Searle to deposit £50 as security for costs. It was hoped amongst Gypsy Lore Society members that Searle wouldn't be able to 'put up' the £50 and the matter would fizzle out. Perhaps it did.

In February 1914 Searle moved his club to a cellar in a house in Regent Street. The press were invited to the event and there were reports of a rustic stile set amongst shingle and a 'kind' of caravan where a gypsy woman was telling fortunes by candlelight. The *Daily Chronicle* reported that those who had turned up wearing evening dress were 'hustled into a dark lobby where they were supplied with shabby suits'.

Rather unkindly, a Gypsy Lore Society member commented later that one of Mr Searle's star guests on the occasion, a Miss Winifred Borrow, was a third-rate actress whose connection with George Borrow was 'very problematical'!

World War I brought an end to the petty warring between the two clubs, as gypsiologists were called up to serve in various ways. For example Scott Macfie, in spite of his forty-six years, joined the British Expeditionary Force of the Liverpool Scottish, and Alice Gillington worked for a farmer in Lulworth haymaking and harvesting. From that time the Gypsy and Folklore Club seems to have folded completely.

The Gypsy Lore Society started again in 1922, and in the years that followed there were various notable events. In 1931 one of its most distinguished members, John Sampson, died; at a moving ceremony conducted by Augustus John, his ashes were scattered to the four winds from a Welsh mountain top. Augustus John wore a red, flowing scarf, red being a Romany colour for mourning. Present were Sampson's family, friends (gypsy and non-gypsy) and the press; when the ashes casket had been emptied, one of Sampson's oldest gypsy friends, Ithal Lee, burnt it. A copy of The Order of the Last Rites can be seen overleaf.

In 1938 the Gypsy Lore Society celebrated its fiftieth anniversary, and there was a Jubilee dinner in Liverpool. Much of the planning and organisation for this was done by Esmeralda Locke's friend, Dora Yates: Miss Yates had been a long-time, much valued member of the society and was then its honorary secretary. The menu for the dinner was witty, for example offering salmon 'boiled, but not poached'. There were gypsy guests, and distinguished gypsiologists came from abroad especially for the event. Augustus John, then president, was unable to attend and so Lady Eleanor Smith took his place. Lady Eleanor, thirty-six at the time, was a writer; she was attractive, with a rather thin face and curly dark brown hair. She proposed the toast – 'To our gypsy guests' – and expressed her thanks to gypsies because she earned her living by writing about them.

Eleanor's brother was the 2nd Earl of Birkenhead. Her father, the 1st Earl, had been a brilliant politician; colleagues knew him as 'F.E.', and he became one of the youngest Lord Chancellors ever appointed. 'F.E.' was friendly with the Duke of Marlborough, and as a girl, Eleanor had spent Christmases at Blenheim Palace, waited on by richly clad footmen,

ORDER OF THE LAST RITES

1. Procession of Gypsies and other friends from LLANGWM to the slopes of FOEL COCH. Mourning will not be worn.

2. On arrival at the appointed place AUGUSTUS EDWIN JOHN will say with a loud voice :—

> 'Obeying his last wishes we, his friends, bear hither the ashes of JOHN SAMPSON in order that, scattered over the slopes of this beautiful mountain, they may become part of the land he loved and rest near the remnant of the ancient race for whom he lived. We build no monument, we inscribe no stone to bear his name. Long will he live in our hearts : longer still in the great work he has done. Mourn we must that never again can we take by the hand the most faithful of friends ; yet we rejoice that he was sent among us to be our companion in sorrow and in joy, to protect from decay our old traditions, and to enrich the world's store of learning.'

3. MICHAEL TREVISKEY SAMPSON will cast the ashes to the winds.

4. AUGUSTUS EDWIN JOHN will continue :—

> ' " Phūv si dindilī pâlē kī phūv, čār kī čār, tha'u čik k'ō čik." Our friend's last wishes have been fulfilled. Let each of us repeat the words he wrote when another Romano Rai, very dear to him, passed away :

> > " 'Parl o tamlo Merimásko Pāni
> > Dava tuki miro vast, tha so
> > Tū kamésas tirē kokoréski
> > Mai kamáva—Te sovés mīstó ! " ' '

5. All, raising their hands in blessing, will repeat :

> 'Te sovés mīstó ! '

6. A harper will play while the assembled friends stand respectfully with uncovered heads.

7. The procession will return to LLANGWM, and drive thence to Cerrig-y-druidion where a meal will be served and the musicians will play.

Lady Eleanor Smith

their hair set with violet powder and flour. Tennis parties at her own home were often graced by the Duke of York (later George VI).

With such a rarefied background it might seem odd that as the Jubilee dinner progressed, Eleanor boasted of her own gypsy descent. It was a claim she frequently made, saying that her great-grandmother Bathesheba was a gypsy. In later years Eleanor's brother Freddie, the 2nd Earl, wrote of her vivid imagination; he described Bathesheba as a stern nonconformist schoolmistress, but one day their father had idly mused of Bathesheba in Eleanor's presence: 'I sometimes wonder if she can have had any gypsy blood in her?' The idea that this could be so took root in Eleanor's head, and later she wrote a story in which she alleged the Duke of Marlborough, finding that her father had quartered four horses at Blenheim without informing him, said: 'You're a damned scoundrel F.E., a damned horse-thieving scoundrel of a gypsy!'

Freddie, younger than Eleanor and always close to her, accepted her gypsy theory, and when their father died, referred to it in the biography he wrote on the 1st Earl. Winston Churchill wrote a foreword to this book and later reproduced the story in his work *Great Contemporaries*. In turn that book found its way to Nazi Germany, and when World War II ended, papers were found which showed Hitler's intention to exterminate the Birkenhead family because of their impure gypsy blood! Although this sounds an unlikely story, I was fortunate enough to have it confirmed by Eleanor's niece, Lady Juliet Townsend. Laughing ruefully she admitted: 'I was only about three at the time, but my name was there on the list!'

Eleanor's childhood home is still owned by the family, and Lady Juliet showed me the library where Eleanor, at the age of nine, made a discovery which inspired her interest in gypsies from that day forward. It had happened on a rainy day when Eleanor, unable to play outside, was wandering round the library; a book with the odd title of *Lavengro* caught her eye, and she took it down and began to read – it was George Borrow's story of gypsies, published in 1851. In her autobiography written eighteen years later, Eleanor said: 'I find it difficult, even now, to describe the extraordinary impression produced on me by this book... the reading of which was to change my entire life... and made me realise, beyond any doubt, that my existence would in future, be somehow bound up with that of the Gypsy people. I had never heard, until then, of the Romani language. In Borrow's book it was printed for me in black and white... I did not guess then, that I, myself, had gypsy blood.'

Eleanor went on to read George Borrow's other gypsy books, and secretly taught herself Romani from them. Some weeks later a family of gypsies parked their caravan about two miles from her home. Eleanor set off with the dawn to find and talk to them. They weren't up when she got to their vardo, and when finally they stirred, they regarded her at first with curiosity, and then ignored her, getting on with their task of preparing breakfast. Unable to contain herself a moment longer, Eleanor launched into a speech of welcome (in her newly acquired Romani), avowing she would always take the part of the Romani against the gajo. They looked amazed – as it turned out they were foreign gypsies, so probably didn't totally understand her; nevertheless the ice was broken, and they laughed and invited her to have breakfast with them.

The gypsies' road onwards to Bicester went by Eleanor's house and so they took her home, ecstatically happy and seated on the vardo beside the driver. When they got near she prayed: 'Please God, let everybody be in the street to see me arrive… please let Freddie be there, too…'

In the ensuing years Eleanor held to her promise that she'd keep faith with gypsies. She included them and championed them in her books, and when in 1937 a new by-law forbade van-dwellers to camp on Epsom Down and thereby excluded them from Derby Day, she spoke up strongly against it.

She continued to love Borrow, stating that to read his books was to 'throw open a door that leads straight into fresh air towards a winding road, the wind on the heath, a younger, sweeter, half-forgotten England'. Several of her own books became cinema-screen hits: the

Lady Eleanor Smith with gypsies on Epsom Downs

Modern gypsies leaving Eleanor's home village

film version of her best known novel, *The Man in Grey*, featured James Mason and Stewart Granger; and her novel *Caravan* was being filmed a few weeks before her death in 1945. She was then forty-three.

In addition to loving gypsies, Eleanor had become involved in the worlds of the circus, boxing and theatre. Unfortunately, perhaps owing to a fire at her childhood home some years ago, there are few surviving personal papers relating to her rather extraordinary life. However, when I visited Lady Juliet, she kindly found what she could in an upstairs room, and left me to look through them.

She had not been gone long when I heard her call to me up the stairs, that a gypsy caravan was making its way past the front door. I rushed downstairs. I don't know whether I half-expected to see a thin, brown-haired nine-year-old on the caravan driving seat; in fact I saw nothing. The golden Cotswold street was bare. I set off in my car and after a few minutes came upon two gypsy waggons making a steady but brisk pace. I drew up several hundred yards in front of them and jumped out carrying my camera. The front waggon was being led by a handsome, dark young fellow, walking beside the horse; with the waggon behind were a young woman, a baby and a dog. I asked if I could photograph them, and the young man nodded but never slackened his pace. By the time I'd pressed the shutter, the signpost pointing to Eleanor's home village was slipping away behind them, and very soon the road was empty.

The Gypsy Lore Society continues to this day, but now its headquarters are in America. However, the society's goldmine of archive material is still in Britain, kept in Liverpool (the home of the society for so many years) in the Special Collections and Archives Department of the University library.

PETER INGRAM

'OBeng te lel o bales te covel Kova lili! Augustus E. John.' This is deep Romani and means: 'May the Devil take the bastard that steals this book!'

This is written in the front of a bound volume of Augustus John's Gypsy Lore Society Journals, and it was translated for me by Peter Ingram who now owns them. In fact Peter could add his own name below that of John's, because he feels exactly the same. He is also a romantic at heart; for instance when he dies he wants his ashes scattered from a hilltop, like those of the Gypsy Lore Society's Dr Sampson in 1931. However, unlike Sampson, Peter's chosen spot is not a Welsh mountain, but Hartlebury Ridge in Worcestershire; and he would like the duet from Bizet's 'The Pearl Fishers' to be played during the course of the ceremony. Hartlebury is Peter's childhood home.

He is what gypsies call a 'posh rat' – that is, his father was a gypsy but his mother was a gorgio, a non-gypsy. However, it would be difficult to find any one more steeped in gypsy ways. He also looks Romani, and can tell at a glance who is a traveller and who isn't. For example, a couple of years ago he was on board a plane coming back from Canada when a fellow sat down beside him. They eyed each other surreptitiously for a few moments, both, as it turned out, thinking 'He's a traveller lad!' But nothing was said until Peter decided to break the ice with 'How're you doin' mush?' The chap grinned and replied in kind. He turned out to be a cousin to one of Peter's northern mates, Henry Miller, and they began to talk non-stop about mutual friends amongst northern gypsies, even though it was the first time they'd met. 'Wasn't it strange, that out of all those hundreds of passengers, he should sit by me?' Peter added after he told me this.

When he's not travelling, Peter lives in Selborne, Hampshire. His property in the High Street was once an undertaker's premises, and the yard is useful because there he can build and restore gypsy waggons; there was also room enough to make a museum of gypsy arte-facts. Latterly this has closed down, however, and when I called on Peter one mid-winter morning, his mood matched the weather: 'It's the end of it all now, it's a way of life gone, there are no true travelling gypsies left.' The damp, chilly morning air sat like a blight on the painted vardos in the yard and made the remnants of an open fire overhung by a tall black pot hook look sullen. Peter coughed alarmingly, and it turned out that he was hardly over a bout of 'flu.

Opposite: Peter Ingram playing his 'father's bones'

The next time we met the sun was shining, he was recovered, the vardos were a blaze of beautiful colours, and birds were singing in the trees which stretch behind his premises up to Selborne's famous Hanger wood. Peter showed me into the outer room of his self-built house. A fire was burning merrily in the grate making it almost hot enough to leave the top half of his front door (made by himself on the lines of a waggon door) open. In fact the room gives you the impression you are in the sunny outdoors, for its roofing is transparent material and the walls are all windows.

His whole house is interesting and individual. There is wood carving on the doors, photographs of gypsies from times past on the walls, an assortment of craft artefacts, some fine old furniture and lots of books. Many of the books contain poems of adventure and romance of trapper and gold rush days. Peter reeled off the names of some of their authors: ' "Banjo" Patterson; Henry Lawson; Robert Service, his poem "The Ballard of Barb Wire Bill" is my favourite. Then there's a lot of books written by Archibald Standfeld Belaney who's better known as "Grey Owl". People used to think he was an Indian, but although he actually married one, he wasn't one himself. He wrote about his trapper's life in the Canadian bush and how he turned from trapping to being a conservationist. He's my hero, a man who trod his own path!' He sighed in admiration.

In a massive section on its own are gypsy-related books, one of the best collections I've ever seen. I looked through them whilst he brewed some coffee, and when it was made and poured, he showed me the only item he has which belonged to his father: a pair of bones which his father used to play in the Talbot Hotel at Hartlebury. He gave me a virtuoso, clacking, toe-tapping burst from them before laying them aside. His father was Rupert Ingram and came from Swallow's Nest in Sheffield, and he went to Hartlebury to work, putting up asbestos sheeting on Air Ministry buildings. But ever a rover, he'd left Peter's mother not long after Peter's birth.

Peter remembers his grandparents Marie and Tom Ingram, and recalled the excitement of a train journey when he was three, when his mother took him to visit them in Sheffield. He was thrilled with their pigs, chickens and goats, and was very impressed by his grandmother's shiny black hair. 'It's buttered,' his mother had told him afterwards. We will let Peter take up his own story:

'When I was at the village school in Hartlebury I was the only boy who'd sit next to the gypsy lads. Out of school hours I'd go onto the common where the gypsy caravans and tents were. A little chap called Mannie Locke used to test me on Romani words, and I learnt to make pegs and flowers. I moved out of home when I was about fifteen, and for six years took a civilian carpenter and coach-building apprenticeship in the RAF.

'I was earning 30s a week when I bought my first gypsy caravan, a bow-top – it was the last one on Hartlebury Common. It had been owned by Percy Hodgkins, and he's sold it to old Wisdom Smith – this was at the end of the 1950s, and Wisdom wanted £25 for it. I used to go to see him in the tin hut he lived in; it had an earth floor, bible pictures round the walls and an old stove in the centre. He'd be sat up in bed wearing a plaid shirt and a scarf, triple-wrapped. He had a big moustache. There was a round baby-food tin by his bed which he used as a spitoon; he used to smoke Pigtail twist which made you spit. You used to rub it by pulling two fingers backwards and forwards either side of your thumb.

'He'd say to me: "Have you got the money yet?" One day I told him I'd managed to save up £8 10s, and counted it out in front of him. He picked it up and said, "The waggon is yours, my son." I got harness and coach lamps in as well. 'Wisdom was one of the old-type dandies who'd put wild flowers in their hat-bands or their lapels, and set a row of kiss curls over their forehead with water. He used to have a great chain of sovereigns across his chest when he went out to the pub, and when he was there he'd sit very upright and dignified, smoking a big meerschaum pipe, everyone looking at him. He'd take a few puffs and then hold the pipe away from him so they could all see and admire it. If a stranger came into the pub and up to the bar Wisdom would go up to him and keep whining for a pint until the bloke gave in and ordered him one – but just before he went to pay, Wisdom used to pull a wad of notes from his pocket and say: "For being such a nice kind gent, you're to have these on me."

'At this time I was friendly with the Price family; the father, Stranger Price, had a granny who'd been an Ingram. He's dead now, but I'm proud to have his cap and pipe. Every spring the Prices went from Canton Common in Cardiff up the border to Chester, then to Sandbach and Congleton, then they'd turn and head towards Wolverhampton; then Bransford the other side of Worcester for the hop-picking, then to Usk where they'd stop at the barrel-making works and pick up big barrel hoops for making and repairing their bow-top waggons. After that they'd head back to Canton Common.

'All along their route they'd be calling with pegs and baskets. Most of the baskets were made from willow which they'd order, and which arrived at a station with string round it and a label made out to them, the same as water jacks came. They'd gather wool off barbed wire to make mops, and also sell wild flowers. I can remember old gypsy women picking pillowcases full of cowslips.'

Peter then went on to relate that using his carpentry skills he had made gypsy knife-grinding machines for sale, and in 1963, on Castlemorton Common near Malvern, his first handbuilt waggon which he also sold. The next one he made he kept and travelled in; he showed me a photo of it, and on the side was a board listing the services he offered to interested passers-by. The list indicated his adaptability, because *inter alia* he could supply cherrywood pipes; give zodiac advice; build a waggon; sharpen tools; or provide a dog collar or pot scourer. The pot scourers he made from bits of sheep's wool.

'I sold lace too, that's not on the list. We got it from Jack Cundy of Institute Buildings somewhere

The list that appeared on Peter's waggon

'Chiv Bairer' (knife grinder)

Harry Hall (aged 47) 'When I was a boy me and another boy made one from an old bike, grinding blocks and a pulley. We painted it red and decorated it with yellow scrolls. We used to go round houses, sometimes 600 houses a day asking to sharpen scissors, shears and knives. We charged £2 10s.'

The photographs below show a gypsy knife grinding machine bought two years ago by farmer Eric Freeman (left). He saw it for sale at Stow Horse Fair, and thought it might be something of an attraction if it was displayed at Newent Onion Fair which is held in that Gloucestershire town each September. This machine is a tribute to the gypsy trait for recycling material wherever possible or making something from nothing.

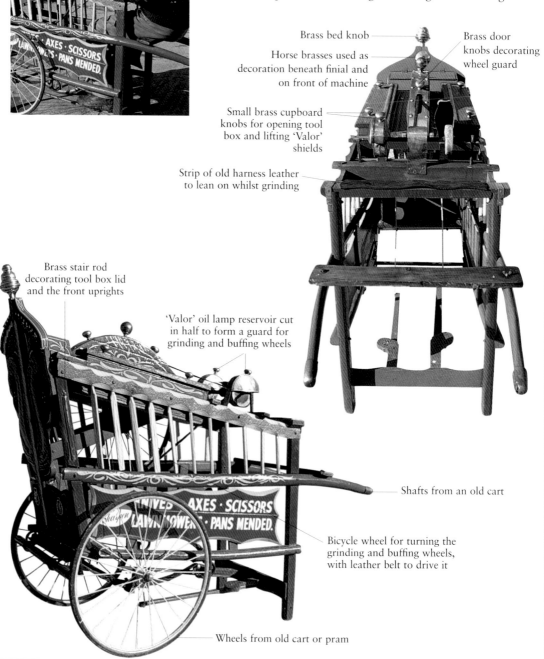

Brass bed knob

Brass door knobs decorating wheel guard

Horse brasses used as decoration beneath finial and on front of machine

Small brass cupboard knobs for opening tool box and lifting 'Valor' shields

Strip of old harness leather to lean on whilst grinding

Brass stair rod decorating tool box lid and the front uprights

'Valor' oil lamp reservoir cut in half to form a guard for grinding and buffing wheels

Shafts from an old cart

Bicycle wheel for turning the grinding and buffing wheels, with leather belt to drive it

Wheels from old cart or pram

in Derbyshire. We'd order a big packet of lace ends for £1 10s and it would come by train, and we'd sort it, put bits onto cardboard and say we'd made it.'

At one point he joined up with gypsies in Dorset. His particular friends were Danny Cooper and his family, which included Eli Hughes. He told me about the hardships of travelling life:

'In the winter the waggons went bitter cold once you were in bed because the old type of stove wouldn't keep in all night. You'd put your water jack by it and there was sufficient warmth to stop that freezing, but the waggon itself would be creaking and cracking with ice.

'We used to take water out of cattle troughs. If the farmer hadn't padlocked the bit with the valve which came direct from the mains we'd drink from that, but if he had, we used to scoop out the leaves and debris from the main body of the tank and drink from there. I remember I got dreadful poisoning once from doing this, vomited and vomited, but it didn't affect the rest of the gypsies at all.

'The police would frequently move us on, and this was irritating when you were tired and hungry and perhaps hadn't sold much that day. Eli Hughes used to say to the policeman, "Have you got a photograph of yourself, Sir?" and the policeman would ask "Why?" and he'd answer, "To put up in me waggon because I likes you, my dear man." That was called "moodying" because it made the policeman laugh – we still had to move off, but it made the atmosphere better. We were often turned out of pubs, or the landlord would say,

'Moodying'

"You can have one, but you've got to go when the locals come in."

'But there's one thing we could do then which you couldn't today without risk of theft, and that was to leave our waggons, water jacks and harness unattended all day on the verge when we went calling. It would all be untouched when we got back. Mind you, we always left a dog chained up.

'Of course gypsies themselves weren't always strictly lawful; for instance some had motor vehicles, and they'd put a Guinness bottle label inside their windscreen instead of an excise licence – it was round, you see, and looked like a licence disk! It wasn't unknown, either, for a smart young gypsy who'd passed his own driving test to take tests for his mates. He'd go along to the test centre and give their name.

'When I was in Dorset I wanted to go and see some gypsies at Canford Heath, but the local gypsies warned me against it – "poverty people" they called them. But I went nevertheless, and Danny Cooper went with me. They were kind enough when we got there, invited us in and offered us tea out of jam jars. I sat down and drank mine. But on the way back Danny kept away from me, saying, "Mush, you got joovers [lice]!" – and I had, too! I went to the chemist to get some sulphur candles, and when I asked for them, a lady standing next to me took twenty steps back!'

Peter laughed, and scratched at the memory. Then his face became serious: 'The Prices and Coopers were people who couldn't move with the times, the old type, travelling at the tail end in the fifties and sixties. No one wanted wooden pegs then, blacksmiths couldn't come out to shoe horses, and you couldn't get a waggon wheel repaired. It's different now, it's all become popular again.'

I knew he was an expert on gypsy clothes, so asked if he'd show me some of the ones he'd collected for his museum. Despite his vast knowledge of male gypsy fashion (he's made a video about it, covering the years 1900 to 1950), we started first with women's clothing. He held up a black pinny: 'Gypsy women either made their own, or they sent to a Mrs Green in Birmingham for one. It fastened by crossing over at the back. On the front are horse-shoe-shaped pockets, and inside are big begging pockets – "mongiputsis" – which, as the day went on, got fatter because when calling a woman might say, "Have you got a few bits and pieces for the babby?" and would generally be given an item or two. They might have a "monging gunner" too, that's a nice clean sack slung across the shoulders.'

An apron would be worn over the pinny; Peter showed me a bright red spotted one, voluminous with the generous length of material it contained. He said: 'Like this one, they usually had a saddle front, that is, the wide waistband would dip into a "V" at the front. A woman would also carry a basket when she went out calling, and it would have straps to help her carry it when it was heavy.'

To look at menswear we went out of the house and across the yard where Peter's museum pieces are stored. He obligingly lifted up a dummy dressed in men's clothes, and clearing a path through the remains of a display on bender tents (he's also made a video on

Opposite: Poacher's pockets

106

gypsy tents), brought it out into the daylight of the yard so that I could see it better. We started by looking at the red scarf round the neck. He explained: 'Men wore their dicklo [scarf] crossed, with each end tied to the opposite braces. Shirts were usually Union-type ones, that is, with a flannel panel in front for warmth. Keeping warm was important, and that's why waistcoats were long and trousers were cut so that they were very high up the back. The trousers were usually leg-of-mutton style, a bit like breeches, that is, wide at the top but narrow in the lower leg. They were lined with swan's down, again for warmth 'cos men didn't wear underpants, and they were made using lap seams, that's seams which over-lap. Trouser pockets were big enough to take white fivers.

'Jackets had four arch shapes, or yokes, on the back across the shoulders, and had lap-and-strap seams. They had five biggish pockets on the outside and one big poacher's pocket inside. Jacket and trousers were known as "suits" even if they didn't match. Different tailors used to make them up specially for the gypsies, and timed their sale to around, say, the end of hop-picking when they knew the gypsies got paid.'

Lastly we looked at the pair of boots in which the model was quite realistically stood astride. I was delighted when Peter called them 'Luton' boots, because several travellers had spoken of having worn this sort of boot, but didn't have any to show me; moreover the last one-time-Luton-boot-wearer I'd talked to thought that their makers had ceased trading about twenty-five years previously because their skilled workforce had died out. The boots on the model were brown leather, but across the middle of the foot there was a broad black band which tapered away up to the ankle. Separating the brown from the black was a strip of brown brogue, but beneath that, and showing through the punched holes, was brilliant

Luton boots

red leather. Well, it had once been bright, but the years had dimmed it on this pair. Nevertheless, polished up, the boots would still have made very showy footwear.

'Why are they called Luton?' I asked.

'Because they came from a Luton factory. You could have button-sided, elastic-sided or high-legged boots with laces, all mostly brogued. I saw a wonderful pair on a traveller boy in the 1960s. I wish I'd asked to buy them.'

We stopped for chunks of new bread and cheese and peach chutney washed down by mugs of tea. Peter talked of drinking tea with Mena Lee at Appleby Fair years ago: 'Her father was Oliver Lee, Ithall's brother. The Lees were Welsh royal gypsies, and it was like taking tea with the Queen.'

He also told of some stories he'd written down, of happenings amongst the gypsies in the 1950s and 1960s; at the time he'd written them like a diary, but each told a story. He read bits to me, and my immediate reaction was: 'They're marvellous, write some more and make a book.' He shrugged.

I hope he does, but I think instead he'll work on his plans for re-opening his yard as a centre for gypsy workshops and craft courses; he will sell his videos, and carry on talking to schools about a way of life disappeared from the countryside. And when he's not doing all that he'll read *Grey Owl*, and poetry by Robert Service, and the gypsy blood in him will yearn to be away somewhere. His faded brown Canadian backpack with its strip of red binding round the top is always close to hand; it's his only luggage because he likes to travel light, and hates waiting by suitcase carousels. Well, maybe he'll take it and go off to Canada where, by courtesy of one of his trapper friends, an untamed tract of land is waiting for him.

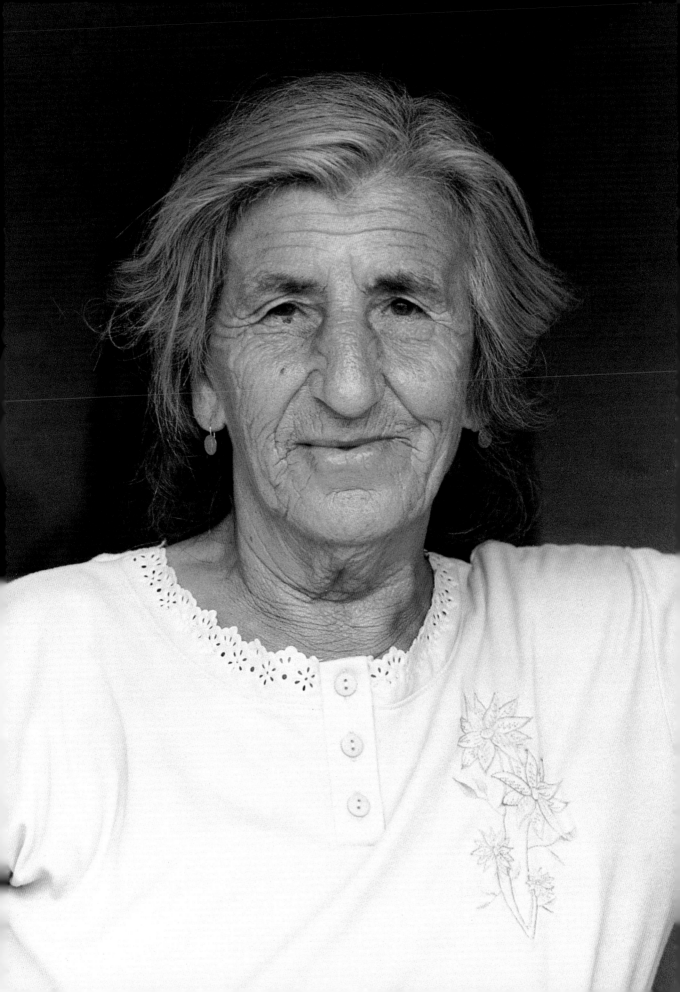

VIOLET SMITH

Last summer I had a rather disturbing experience. I had been with my friend, Violet Smith, an Oxfordshire gypsy, to visit her husband's grave. On the way back we stopped at a town to do some shopping and, returning to the car, we passed a sign which simply said 'Town Museum'; we both decided we'd like to look round. The museum was upstairs in one large room. We went in and started to work our way round the exhibits when a sharp voice called out to us that we hadn't paid. This was a surprise, because there had been no mention of an entrance fee on the board downstairs, or on the outside door. I hastily put matters right, but was annoyed because it would surely have been fairer to have advertised the fact that payment was required.

I was also annoyed at being spoken to in such a peremptory way. I admit I looked nothing special in my old jeans, but Violet was very smart in her dark blazer, black skirt and lovely jumper. However, her dark hair in its loose bun, her gold earrings and her strong features, all clearly denoted her Romani origins, and as I paid I did wonder whether discrimination was the reason for this hostile attitude. I didn't like it, and felt too angry to enjoy the rest of our visit. Violet, however, perhaps through good manners, let the incident pass, and expressed genuine interest in the items; in particular she liked the models of horse-drawn waggons.

In fact Violet is able to rise above prejudice, and the following incident that she described to me just goes to prove this: she had officially opened the gypsy camp site where she is now living, and the ceremony on television showed her talking to the mayoress. The next day when she was in the local market people were pointing at her and saying, 'There's that gypsy that was on TV!' She had turned to them and said simply: 'I am proud to be a gypsy.'

Violet has been on that caravan site for two or three years. She helps to keep an overall eye on matters there and is consulted over prospective residents; she is also responsible for issuing electricity cards to site holders. It's a pleasant place, and the more so for Violet as two of her sons and a daughter are her immediate neighbours. Flower borders surround the hard standing on which her caravan rests, bright with roses and tall, deep yellow sunflowers; Violet likes flowers and told me that when her trailer was in a lay-by for a number of years she built a rockery beside it. It attracted a lot of attention from passing motorists!

Although now settled in Oxfordshire, Violet originates from Yorkshire. She was born in

Opposite: Violet Smith

her parents' 'Reading' caravan at Doncaster, and was one of eight children. Her mother was Rhoda Smith, and like her brothers and sisters, Violet kept the surname Smith because Rhoda never married their father whose surname had been Egerton. He'd dealt in horses, and sold brown stew-pots which he picked up from the kilns and carried on a flat-cart.

The family travelled in two waggons. If they came to a hill they put a 'side-liner' onto the waggon, to help pull it up the gradient. More usually known as a 'sider', this was a horse brought from the back waggon and fastened with harness and traces beside the shafts of the horse already pulling.

They left Yorkshire when Violet was twelve years old. World War II had started the previous year, and Violet remembers food rationing: 'People who lived in houses had to register with certain shops in their area, but travellers like ourselves had special ration books which allowed us to call at shops wherever we were. But at a butcher's, say, you'd join a long queue, and when finally you got to the counter they wouldn't give you anything, they'd say they were keeping things for their regulars. But we didn't do too badly, we got milk, potatoes and other veg from the farmers. I used to ride a pony bareback down to farms we stopped near and collect the milk. I brought it back in a galvanized container strapped to my waist.

'In the evenings we used to listen to the wireless. I loved the Dick Barton serials, and if they were on and I got asked to make a cup of tea I used to say to my dad "Turn it off until I come back, so I won't miss anything!"

Violet spent some of her childhood with her mother's sister-in-law Aunt Charlotte up in Doncaster. She explained why this was: 'I had to have an operation, and Aunt Charlotte paid for it by selling lavender. When I came out of hospital I went to live with her. I still go up to see her, she buys me a rail ticket and sends it; I help when they go to Doncaster races – her son takes some ponies and tack and gives rides near the course, and Aunt Charlotte tells fortunes. She's very well known for her fortune-telling; she's known as "Madam Smith" and has a trailer at Appleby Fair amongst the fortune-tellers. People who've been to her before always ask for her again because she tells them what they want to know. She'll make your hair stand on end, it's a gift – clients even ring her up from America. She told Prince Charles's fortune once. She was at a "country fayre" on one of his estates and he came to see her.'

Violet's husband, now sadly deceased, was Jabez Smith. They'd met at Lichfield where her granny had a yard. 'Mum and Dad went off in the horse-drawn waggon and I was left looking after Granny, who was stone-deaf. There were other family about, uncles and aunts. I went to the pictures with some of them and that's where I met Jabez. We ran off three weeks later and got married at Alcester. We earned a living by doing jobs like pea-picking in the Vale of Evesham, and I didn't get in touch with Mum and Dad for months. We went back eventually. It's not unusual for gypsy girls to run away with boys. They do it because their parents are so strict about them having boyfriends. Two of my daughters eloped. But if a girl runs away with a man and he doesn't marry her and leaves her, the parents won't have her back because she's lain with a man.'

When Violet told me this I remember I said that it seemed harsh, because if a girl had been deserted then that was the time she needed her family. But Violet was adamant that she'd remain banned. 'It's our way,' she said. Nevertheless, I remain puzzled over this strict code, because Violet is almost obsessional in her love for her children even though they're grown up and parents themselves. Moreover it's a two-way feeling, for she says that they never leave her except to go on short holidays, and even then they ring her and soon come back.

Violet also described Jabez's relationship with the children – 'Jay', as she used to call him: 'He was very strict, but he never hit 'em. He always had his meals before they had theirs, and if they were around and he wanted peace and quiet, or to talk to someone, he only had to make a slight movement with his eyes and they melted away. He never went to any of their weddings. He said, "I don't believe in giving my children away."'

Violet has seventeen grandchildren and was present at the birth of each one; she goes to the hospital and helps the nurses during the delivery because it is what her daughters and daughters-in-law want. In fact, not long ago a complete stranger who had come to live on the caravan site went to hospital to have a baby and sent her husband with the urgent message for Violet: 'Get me out, Violet, they're killing me!' I'd read that it was a gypsy custom to put a portion of straw under their women when they were having babies in hospital, and that doctors and nurses allowed this, but Violet said that this was not true.

When any of her grandchildren start school Violet goes with their mother to see the headteacher. 'We tell them that the children are never to be caned, and they're not to have any sex education. At home they're not allowed to watch videos which have sex scenes. Girls aren't told about periods either, it's considered to be dirty. I remember that when I was first "taken poorly" I was on a waggon with my cousin, a girl older than myself, and she explained to me what was happening.'

Violet considers Friday to be an unlucky day, and described sad events such as family deaths and misfortunes which had happened on Fridays. Owing to its unluckiness they never moved camp on Fridays.

She talked to me at length about her travelling days; 'travel for the callin' was her phrase: 'I used to sell flowers and pegs. The pegs were made by someone during the day at the camp out of nut or willow. Willow was best because you could "mouth" it better. The flowers were like chrysanthemums and made out of elderberry wood. We'd break off some privet because it kept green, and push it into the middle of the flower-head like a stem, and stand 'em in water. We made chrysanths and carnations out of crêpe paper, too. Mops was another thing. We'd make the heads from threads drawn from old hessian sacks, then get a long willa' stick and put a piece of leather back and front of the mop-head and nail it to the stick.

'We were always polite, never pushy when we knocked on doors; in fact my father told me, "If a lady gives you a pot of jam or half-a-dozen eggs, always give her some pegs or flowers in return and you'll never get into trouble." Another thing he used to say was: "My baby, always keep a clean pair of sheets and nightclothes in case you have to have the doctor."

'Well, we used to work us way down to the hopfields. There'd be farmers' tatters, swedes, sugar beet or mangolds to lift and we even bagged up elderflowers for sale. If we got to the hopfields and they weren't quite ready for picking we'd work round about till it was time to pull in. One thing about hops was they gave you an appetite, and there'd be kippers, lardy cakes and doughnuts being sold every day in the hopfields.'

On the subject of food I asked Violet if she ever made any jams and chutneys. She didn't, but she told me that her dad's mum used to make rosebud jam and also blackberry wine. Jabez's favourite jam had been damson, but never on a ready-sliced loaf: 'lazy-woman bread' he called that, Violet explained. Traditional food is valued, and when Violet goes to Doncaster to Aunt Charlotte's she goes to the shop where her aunt always buys bread because here, corned beef is still made 'as it used to be', also black puddings; and she stocks up with plenty to bring home.

Violet admitted to me that although she has travelled extensively, she has never been on water – in fact she saw the sea for the first time about three years ago. It didn't make a tremendous impact on her, and she hadn't even wanted to go onto the beach. But her father when he was a young man had often gone across the water to Ireland: 'I remember him telling the tale of how dogs weren't allowed on board the ferry. He'd had a greyhound which had been with him some time in Ireland and the dog went down to the boat with him, but he had to leave it on the dockside. As the ferry pulled out he saw an elderly man take hold of it, and Dad waved his hand to him to say thank you.'

When I asked Violet which bit of her life she had liked best, she said: 'Field-work, because you could be sure of the money – knocking on doors you didn't know.' In later years she'd been a forewoman on a farm which grew market produce, and had been responsible for giving out the wages. Talking of honesty and trust, she said: 'We always brought up our children not to touch what isn't theirs.' She had gestured to my car, at the time parked outside her trailer, and had said: 'You need have no fear that any of my family's children will touch it – but if you turned up and I wasn't in, they'd soon come over and ask what you wanted; it's the way they've been brought up.'

When she and Jabez stopped travelling they had settled their trailer in a lay-by outside Chipping Norton, and Violet had started keeping Shetland ponies. Eventually she had about sixty of them, including a stallion, kept in various fields which she rented. Jabez took no part in this, preferring his own interest which was birds, particularly pigeons. He loved them so much that the family has put statues of fantailed pigeons and game cocks on his grave.

It is sadly fitting that Jabez's name is allied in the Bible to sorrow, for Violet mourns him deeply. They had been married for forty-five years when he died in 1990 aged sixty-six. Violet says proudly: 'He never laid his hand on me – was never jealous – would never go over the road without me. Other women used to say "I wish my husband was like that." He said that if anything happened to me he couldn't live without me.'

For nine months whilst he was in Warwick Hospital she never left his side, sitting and sleeping in a chair beside the bed: 'If I hadn't been there, he wouldn't have stayed.' The family brought him home when he died, and sat up with him all night before the funeral.

Many other waggons belonging to friends and relatives turned up and parked next to Violet's, and their occupants also sat up all night. Violet has clear and lasting memories of Jabez's funeral:

'It was huge – I was asked if it could be filmed, but I refused. I requested that on the way to the church the cortège make a special detour to the bus depot where there was a café. You see, it had always been Jabez's custom to have tea and a bacon sandwich there when I was doing shopping in the town. As a mark of respect the café was closed that day, and all the employees were outside with wreaths.

'There were wonderful tributes. Some people brought birds and cages made in flowers, and my daughter had a floral replica made of Jabez's lorry, complete with number plate; later, when the flowers faded, she kept the wire and had a wooden lorry made which we put on the grave – but it was taken off several times, so we brought it back here and now it's on his actual lorry. I won't let anyone drive his lorry.'

I knew that an especially favoured floral tribute on a gypsy grave is an arch with gates beneath and steps leading up to them, known as 'The Gates of Heaven'; I didn't know what this meant, so asked Violet to explain the tribute and the implication behind it. She said: 'The gates are closed when it's put onto the grave. If later the gates are open, then the deceased has gone up to heaven; if they are only half open, then he or she has not.'

Violet Smith tends her husband's grave

Violet has kept Jabez's personal possessions. 'When I'm gone they'll be burnt, and any bits left in the ashes will be scooped up and buried in a pit somewhere.' Every day for four years she went to Jabez's grave, and even tried to get some permanent living accommodation in the local town, but couldn't. She then used to walk thirteen miles to and from the cemetery several times a week. The grave is impressive, and beautifully kept; moreover Violet has bought the adjoining plot so that it can't be blocked off. She doesn't allow the local authority to mow either plot in case they damage the stone, but instead she pays someone to mow both plots. She has bought a wooden and wrought-iron seat, and put it on the grass nearby; she spends many hours sitting here, and knows the other visitors to that part of the cemetery well, now.

The family still remains close to Jabez. They go to the grave to see in the New Year, and when the last grandchild was born, despite it being twelve at night, Violet's son went to the cemetery to tell his father about the baby and to hang a little chain and cross 'for the baby' on the grave. Unfortunately this was later stolen.

Next to her trailer Violet has a large cage for Jabez's three birds: two goldfinch mules and a goldfinch. She looks after them tenderly. If I visit her I try to remember to take some groundsel for them, as they love its yellow, half-opened buds. I took a bunch of it to Stow Fair because I knew I'd meet Violet – it was one of Jabez's last wishes, that she should always go there.

Gypsy cures

Violet Smith of Oxfordshire: 'If a baby's bound up, boil some
groundsel and give it a little on a teaspoon. It will open the bowels.'

'For earache, boil an onion and get the thin piece out of the
centre, hold it in the ear. Or put a bit of baccy in the ear or blow
smoke down the ear.'

THE COULSONS OF
CRAGHEAD

꧁꧂

Outside the town of Appleby in Cumbria there is a hill, and at Horse Fair time in June hundreds of caravans spread over it, a mixture of both the trailer kind and picturesque old vardos. Scores more park on the verges of the town's approach roads. On this occasion I wandered around amongst the hill vans in the half-light of early evening; there was laughing and talking, women hanging out tea-towels to dry, and vans which appeared to be family groups. I knew not a soul. I walked by a large roped-off area designated for Christian gypsies, and came across a section where caravans were still arriving, many pulled by impressive four-wheel-drive vehicles.

One family, however, had gone no further than the approach way, and had parked their caravan under the hedge. Beside it there was a stick fire burning, and around it were a young boy, a stockily built man in his forties, an older man, and stretched in front of them on the grass, a youth. I plucked up the courage to say that I was interested in talking about gypsies' lives in former years, and to ask if I could talk to them. The older man melted away into the dusk, the boy went off to play, the youth remained stretched out on the ground, and the middle-aged man answered me civilly. He sat on a straw bale, and the light from the fire illuminated his big sad eyes and moustache. He was wearing a trilby hat, grey striped trousers, a waistcoat and a neckerchief. He said to me: 'There are hawkers, gypsies and travellers, and my family

Ada Coulson,
a 'black-faced' gypsy

are hawkers, always have been – but my wife is a pure gypsy, one of the black-faced Boswells.'

It turned out that the youth was also a Boswell, but they hadn't met until a short time before; he was from Manchester and was trying to find out about his ancestry. And I learned that the man on the bale was Warren Coulson, '...from County Durham. My wife will talk to you.' At that point Mrs Coulson came out of the caravan. She was young, and not in the least black-faced – in fact her complexion was very pale, but she had jet-black eyes and hair. Her husband explained who I was, and I was invited into the caravan.

Mrs Coulson told me that her name was Ada, short for Abrada. Also in the caravan were her daughter Katy Abrada (aged about thirteen) and her baby grandson Jack, son of her daughter Tanya who was arriving on the following day. At thirty-five, Ada was the

117

*Charlotte Smith and her
husband Henry*

youngest grandmother I'd ever met. She told me that she, too, was trying to find out about her Boswell ancestors. Her grandparents were Jack and 'Nation (Carnation) Boswell, but her surname had been Wood: her father's name had been Laurence Wood, and her mother's had been Violet Smith; her grandmother on her mum's side, Charlotte Smith, lived in Doncaster. I nearly dropped my cup of tea when I heard this, because Charlotte Smith was the aunt of my friend Violet from Oxfordshire – that is, her mother's sister-in-law. Ada, being Charlotte's daughter's girl, would be Violet's great-niece. I asked Ada if she knew Violet, but she shook her head.

Ada went on to tell me that Violet her mother had died when she was five months old. She and her three brothers and two sisters had lived with their father, Grannie 'Nation and her father's sister Tilly, whose proper name was Celia; another of her father's sisters, Wickie, had spent a lot of time with them, too. Granny 'Nation died when Ada was ten, and her father died seven months later. In Ada's own words: 'We lived in a house at Coxhoe, then moved to neighbouring Wingate. Aunt Tilly brought us up strict. We weren't allowed to go anywhere and had no real friends, though we did go to fairs. We'd take the waggon, an open lot, and a trailer, and Aunt Tilly told fortunes; she still does, and is here now at Appleby – she's deaf, but she can lip-read. When she's at home she still goes out every day, rain, snow or shine, knocking on doors selling flowers and telling fortunes. She goes on the bus and takes her wares in a cardboard box – she goes out at six or seven in the morning, and comes back at eight or nine at night. She makes the flowers – though when I lived with her I had to make the flowers of a night-time.

*Grannie 'Nation, in spotted scarf,
surrounded by friends and family*

'She always drummed into us girls to keep away from lads and men. When I left school I went to work in a factory which made cuddly toys, and I met a local man and married him. About eight months later we were coming here to Appleby for the fair and pulled in for the night near the Sun Inn. The next morning I found him dead beside me; he'd died of a heart complaint. No one stays at that stopping place now, I don't know whether that's coincidence.

'I got together with Warren on the day that Princess Diana got married. He's a good man. When we go anywhere we stay on our own. I won't go where there's close neighbours, we keep away from trouble.'

Ada gave me her address in County Durham and said I was welcome to visit; I promised to send anything I could find about Boswells in old books about gypsies. The next day I saw

Aunt Tilly over the half door of her vardo. The vehicle was stately, old-fashioned and beautiful in green, cream and gold paint. Aunt Tilly was 'Mother Egypt' personified, quite the darkest gypsy I'd ever seen. She was taking a rest from fortune-telling so I didn't disturb her; I hope we meet one day.

I did meet Ada and her family again. In the autumn I was near County Durham, and I booked into the Punch Bowl pub at Craghead so that I could call on them the next day. The pub is at a crossroads on high ground, perhaps the 'crag head' of the village name. Behind it are rows of terraced houses, and on the road past it, allotments with pigeonlofts and small pieces of ground where hardy-looking ponies graze; stretching beyond all these are farm fields surrounded by dark stone walls. Craghead was a mining village until the last pit closed in 1968. The pub lounge has old photos of the collieries, and the landlord told me: 'People here still have an affinity for coal.' I was glad to hear it, because Warren, Ada's husband, owned the local coalyard.

I found the yard by driving to the bottom of the hill. A little way behind the coal heap and lifting gear was a big, fairly new bungalow, some stables, and a gypsy caravan. Warren was out, but Ada took me into the spotless house. 'A clean fireplace, clean cooker and clean bed, and you're halfway there,' Ada remarked when I said how nice it all looked. 'I go out for two hours one night in the week, and I'd go mad if I found a cup or dishes in the sink when I came back – but I don't, because they'll have been washed and put away. We don't like washing our hands or faces where we do the dishes; we do them in the bathroom or in a spare bowl.'

Ada was minding her grandson Jack whilst her daughter Tanya, who lived in the village with her husband, was at work. Also at home were Katie Abrada, and Ada and Warren's eldest boy Sanchaz (aged fifteen); their brother Duran (ten) was at school. When she's not baby-sitting, Ada often works with a woman friend: 'I take the bairns to school, then I drive the lorry and we work around factories and skips looking for scrap, and between us we load it.' This is her own enterprise, nothing to do with Warren.

Tanya with her horse George

When Warren returned he took me outside to see the gypsy waggon, and told me its history: 'A Durham man called Skinny Hall bought it, and sold it to some tractor agents who sold it on for £900. Next it went on the side of the A1 Gosforth to Morpeth road – it stood as an ornament outside a petrol station, and was there nearly thirty years. I bought it, repaired the base – which is a ninety-year-old Lambert's dray made in Bradford – and got Philip Jowells, the best builder in Britain who lives in Bentham, to make new wheels. The top I completely rebuilt myself. It pulls like a barra,' he added, showing me the van's manoeuvrability by hand-pulling the shafts. It was a fine piece of work, and already sold. I photographed Warren and Sanchaz in it.

There were other horse-drawn vehicles parked round about. Some were vehicles his sons Sanchaz and Duran used for road racing, and I asked Warren to explain to me what

this involved: 'It usually happens at seven in the morning, and we always change venues so the police can't pin us down. It can be just two racing, perhaps with flat carts and road horses. People gamble between themselves on the winner. A point's set on the road or at the side of the road and the two gallop up to that point and when they get there you shout "Off"; any traffic follows behind. Afterwards we go to breakfast, could be fifty of us.'

Warren then showed me his father's flat cart which is kept under cover. His father had run the coalyard and a rag-and-bone business. 'If you want to hear about how that was years ago you should talk to me brother Terry, he's nine years older than me. Sanchaz will take you over to see Terry, he'll talk to you, he's a boxer and a singer too.'

Terry and his wife Margaret were just driving down their short lane to fetch water when we got there, but said they'd soon be back. I drove on, past the place-name 'Romany Way' mounted on posts, and waited by their living trailer. Parked nearby was an old-fashioned gypsy caravan, and round about were various wooden buildings for horses. The surrounding field was divided into sections for grazing, with a group of geese in a central pen.

Terry and Margaret were soon back, and not in the least put out that I'd arrived without warning. Margaret was wearing a colourful jumper and her black skirt was quite long, a style favoured by gypsies. However, she is not of gypsy stock: an attractive, tall, pale redhead, she is the great-great-great-granddaughter of John Peel,

Terry feeding his geese
Top left: the decorative interior of the open lot and (below) Warren and Sanchaz sitting outside
Right: Margaret and Terry

the famous Cumberland huntsman! Busying herself with a kettle on the calor gas stove she explained: 'My great-great-grandmother was Mary Davidson, one of the twin girls amongst John Peel's thirteen children. Her name is on his tombstone in Caldbeck churchyard. Her twin passed away about twenty years ago. I had John Peel's writing desk, but someone stole it. The only thing I've got connected with him is this…' and she lifted a musical box out of a cupboard. 'It isn't his, I bought it off a sale stall somewhere.' The box was old, made of china and decorated with hunting scenes. Margaret set it going and it played 'Do Ye Ken John Peel'.

Terry Coulson had been outside, probably watering the animals; he came in for a cup of tea. He is built sparingly, and bears little resemblance to his brother Warren; he is also, I was to find

out, a good talker, no doubt because he was used to dealing with the public in his rag-and-bone trade, and, in between that, to entertaining on stage as a singer in clubs. On the latter, he's made a cassette recording of his songs, called 'Travelling Man'. Terry was born in 1939 and has had a hard life. He told me about his parentage:

'My grandparents on my mother's side were called Calvert. Grannie had been Margaret Ferguson, she'd married a George Calvert and they called their daughter, my mother, Georgina. My mother met my father, Jack Coulson, when he was out selling.

'During the war I stayed with Mum's parents, but when the war ended Dad took me away to his parents; I was seven at the time, and my childhood ended then. Grandfather Albie Coulson lived at Ashington. Grannie's surname had been Goolie. She'd come from Ireland and they'd met in Scotland where they had a marime yard.'

'What's a marime yard?' I queried.

'For scrap, they took everything. In London it's called "tot", and around here we call it

Grannie Calvert with Tony, one of her grandchildren

a tat shop.' He went on: 'Granddad was a member of the Showman's Guild. He made caravans from hardboard and put them on the beach at Newbiggin-by-the-Sea. He also had a "shaggy" boat roundabout there. Grannie Coulson had a rag-and-bone business. They lived in a big camp with my aunts, and had an old hearse and a boat on wheels.

'The boat had been a proper sea-going one. It had cost £12 and it arrived at the local station. They'd put it onto the springs, turntable and wheels from a Bill Wright dray, so it was a boat on wheels and was pulled about by a horse. It was called *The Victory* and was taken out to collect rags and scrap; after the war there was a tremendous demand for rags. *The Victory* was always kept brightly painted and was high up, eight feet from the ground. You could get forty children in it, a penny a ride. Grannie or Dad used to take the rags out and leave them at the top of the street and take the children to the end of the street and back – that was 400 yards, 200 each way. Once, the boat was escorted outside of Halifax by the police because it was transporting people but didn't have a hackney licence!

'We'd take a ten foot by ten foot square "cottage" tent out in the boat, and pitch it anywhere where there was work and a bit of water near for the horses, then get grafting with the boat. Grannie also went out with a barrow, and Dad took a horse and cart around the Newcastle, Durham and Hexham area. He sometimes used to blow an old army bugle just to make a noise and let people know it was the scrap-man.

'Dad spent three years working with the boat, then peeled away from his parents. He told us boys: "I'm going to learn you how to hawk. First you sell yourself, then the goods,

The Victory, *Grannie Coulson's rag and bone 'cart'*

then the customer's always good." Dad could sell a stone of potatoes to a pensioner who didn't want it.

'Me and my brothers used to sell kippers. A chap called Walter Offit fetched 'em from North Shields, and Dad taught me how to cost a box: count them into one box and average throughout the twenty stone. I had to sell four stone every Monday before school. We'd start selling at six o'clock. The men used to drink on Sunday evenings, and on Monday had kippers for breakfast. Father would give me two streets to do, but whilst I was doing them he'd do four. When he'd gone on his own he took nothing, we didn't have a boat, me and Dad just had a bike but sometimes I didn't even have a bike, just carried the box of kippers. I sold herrings on Tuesdays and fruit on Fridays… I've also sold flowers and muffins and crumpets in my time, but the hygiene regulations stopped the food hawkin'. I'd do miles, then had to be at school at nine o'clock. I was only eleven, but I earned more than the fathers of the other boys at school.

'Sometimes Dad used to hire a horse and cart to collect scrap. He'd get them for 10s a day from Harry Harrap. Mr Harrap had come to Stanley, the town beyond Craghead, with a

Warren with his father's hawking bike

living waggon and opened a scrapyard on some old allotments. In later years he became a millionaire and ended up owning farms too. His son, Ronnie, carries on the business today. Whilst Dad had the horse and cart, we boys used to hire kids' prams at a few pence a day off a tat shop and go round collecting rags, jam jars and 3-gill bottles. The tat shop would give you a shilling for a dozen cleaned-out jam jars, and you could make up to 37s, less the pram money.

'Dad was a hard man. I hated him then, and we never really made it up until two years before he died. When we were children he had his meals first and we had to wait. The more aggressive he got, the more I did too – though funnily enough other lads got on all right with him.

'One day Warren and I were pulling up a bit of fencing for firewood for our mother, and Dad saw it and thought it would be a good thing to sell fire-wood. So we used to have to take pit props away from the mines in a push-chair. Talking about wood-selling, I remember one day when I was with him and Warren, he went to Lord Ridley's estate because there was a wood to be cleared there. Dad took a thousand pounds with him to get the contract to take the horses in and pull out the timber – but then Lord Ridley asked him how much he'd *charge* to clear it, and take it away! So Dad kept the money in his pocket. Unfortunately during the work Warren knocked Lord Ridley's small son's tooth out and his father called Warren a "nasty little boy". But Warren suffered later through wood-selling, because he lost part of one hand in a sawing accident; this happened when he was seventeen.

Terry as a young man

'Opportunities like Ridley's wood really helped things along – in fact the whole busi-ness grew, for by selling kippers Dad saved enough to buy a horse, then we had a chap help us, and then another horse and another workman. Dad had always said, "Before I die they'll call me Mr Coulson!" When he did die, at forty-nine, he'd built up an empire.'

Terry and Margaret's grey and white cat Magic had crept onto my lap when I was lis-tening to Terry, and a little Jack Russell had trotted up the steps and into the trailer; it had been carrying a child's shuttlecock, and was playing with it on the floor. Whilst Terry paused in his story, Margaret introduced the dog:

'This is Candy, and she sings.'

'Will she sing now?' I asked hopefully. Margaret stood up and said: 'Sing, Candy,' and the little dog whimpered slightly and dropped the shuttlecock. 'Sing, Candy!' Margaret commanded again, and the dog sat down in front of her and obediently started to howl.

'Sing, Candy,' repeated Margaret, and raised the pitch of her voice – and so, correspondingly, did Candy. Margaret rewarded her with a chocolate biscuit.

Terry and Margaret's daughter Gina arrived to visit, bringing her children from school; they were excited about a pantomime which they were all in, including Margaret. She opened a cupboard door and showed me their costumes; her own part included a tap dance. She laughed and said, 'I told my mum that when I grew up I was going to be a film star or a gypsy, but my people weren't impressed; they were teachers and doctors and enjoyed hymn-singing evenings.' I remembered the sign to Margaret and Terry's place which said 'Romany Way', and the gypsy caravan nearby and their living in the trailer – and it seemed to me that Margaret had almost achieved her aim. I assumed that the change from a very conventional background to her present lifestyle must have come through Terry, and a little while later she confirmed this. They had met at school when they were both thirteen.

'He turned up at a dance and asked to take me home, to walk me down the road. I agreed, and on the way he said "Do you fancy a bag of chips? Well, give us the money then!" And I immediately thought, "What bad manners!" – but from then on we just clicked: I used to get out of the upstairs window at home to go out with him.

'When I first met him I thought he was the *cruellest* fellow. He used to get his little brothers to kneel down in line in the hall of their house. He'd wrap an old cloth round his fist, then they'd spin a coin to determine who was the first to go down and then he'd jab them under the chin.'

Terry joined in: 'I did it to harden them and teach them to look after themselves. You see, others weren't allowed to associate with us, we were ostracised. It put a chip on your shoulder and you had to be tough to survive.'

Margaret, photographed when a young girl

Margaret: 'He was always protecting his brothers. He'd take off his shirt and fight bareknuckle. He's Scots-Irish with a short fuse, the worst kind of breed you can get for fighting.'

Terry grinned: 'When I was fifteen I told her mam, "I'm going to marry your daughter."'

Margaret: 'It was a Friday when he came to see mother and tell her that. He had a pair of crocodile slippers on with the tongues turned down inside so they looked like shoes. My goodness, he was a proper ragman.'

Terry then went on to tell me that as well as making his marriage plans when he was fifteen, he was given the opportunity to start a singing career. It had happened the following way: 'I was singing in the fish shop, and a member of the Arch Club at South Moor which is nearby here, asked me to sing at venues with him. His name was Joey Smith, he was a homosexual and when he went out to our first show he was wearing lipstick, which was brave in 1954ish. I sang all over, even at the Sunderland Empire when I was sixteen, and won a big talent competition.'

Margaret: 'I was playing for him then. I remember he was so good-looking and I could only play one tune, "Diane", which I did. I had a bridesmaid's dress on and I was shaking. The lassies were screaming at the stage and he was offered a two-year contract, but couldn't take it because of working for his father.

'We had no leisure time when we were courting because of work. I was at his house bathing kids and chopping sticks, for with so many children his mother couldn't do a lot. She was very house-proud. There were no carpets, but all the floorboards were lily white. His father never clouted or shouted, but he kicked and had a wicked temper. We got married when we were both eighteen. Terry had no shirt or suit, so he wore my father's shirt, his brother-in-law's suit and my mother gave him a tie. We had a 10s note on the day to keep us for a week.

'After we married, Warren came to live with us. We only had a tent and my mother, a church person, thought it wasn't decent he should sleep in the tent with us. We made our own living.'

I asked how they'd made money.

Terry: 'I used to box – Warren was still just a little boy, and he used to sit at the ringside and cry when I got hit.'

Margaret: 'There were also "Go as You Please" talent contests in clubs which kept us going for years. We'd get a paper and see where there was one and Terry would go and sing and usually win. Eventually we had a living waggon and a horse and cart, and every summer we used to travel. I drove the flat cart and Terry the living waggon.'

Terry: 'We'd go to, say, Leeds, ask where the rag shop was and get stuff for it, hawk every day.'

It was a business they carried on the rest of the year, too, and Margaret helped even after having her four children. She said, 'I'd put the kids in at school and go tattin' through the day, then pick the kids up and go bullin' the tips at night – that's tin picking, old food tins. I'd load up a horse and cart with as many as I could find and then sold them to the scrapyard so that the waggon would be empty to start next day.'

Terry: 'I'd put handbills through doors, a thousand doors was nowt. These'd say that we'd *buy* non-ferrous

Top: Terry and Margaret: the young courting couple and on their wedding day
Right: Terry with Champ pulling a barrel-top through the town of South Moor, en route to Appleby

metals and we'd *take* any old rags away – one paid for the other. I'd ring a hand-bell to let people know when I was in the street. To encourage the mums to give rags and scrap I'd give out ships and tops, goldfish, windmills, clothes pegs and sandystone for whitening their curbstone outside the door. I used to give out balloons and blow them up, but the health regulations put a stop to all that.

'Pure woollens were classed as "darks, creams and pastels" and we sold them back to the mills at Bradford. Rags were sold as "wipes" to factories.'

Margaret: 'I cut all the buttons and zips off.'

Terry: 'I also used to have customers on my rounds who'd have some of the old stuffin' – scrap and rags is called old stuffin'. It was like a secondhand shop, they'd come out to see if there

Margaret driving a cart which has been decorated for a local parade
Below: Salvaging sea coal at Lynemouth to supplement their income

was anything they wanted on the cart; or they'd say to me, "Look out for a little carpet or a pair o' sheets", or I'd get a topcoat for a client. Sometimes you did a "call-back" – that was when you'd call and the woman would say "There's two copper boilers, come back when my husband gets home." So you made a cross mark with chalk on her door.

'We were out six days a week stuffin', and you could guarantee that on one day a week there'd be a "tickle", which was a hell of a good load. That is, a couple of copper boilers, a nice bit of brass or nice scrapmetal bath.

'At first we spraff'd this sort of thing, meaning begged them, but when we had to pay the profit went down. TV and newspaper advertising of scrapyards giving their prices killed the ragman's life; people used to take their own to the scrapyards. Also by the 1960s there was no selling jam jars and there were no 3-gill bottles. Years ago glass was washed and reused, now it's broken and recycled. The demand for rags also went down, and there became no such thing as woollens.'

To supplement their income Terry and Margaret went salvaging sea coal at Cresswell above Lynemouth on the Northumberland coast. The coal came from a nearby colliery which used to tip its waste coal into the sea. 'I'd known about the colliery since I was a kid,' Terry explained, 'because it was near to where Granddad had his "shaggy" boat roundabout.

'Like other coal salvagers we lived in a

Terry and Margaret with their grandchildren, Joanne Leigh and Georgina and (right) Warren with Sanchaz and Prince, the prized coloured yearling

trailer on the beach. Your patch was marked out and it was known as a "stint on". When the tide came in, it washed the coal up and you shovelled it onto a cart and left it on the shore in heaps. It was sold to a man who owned the rights off the Crown to retrieve coal. Sometimes the coal might come in on a tide at two o'clock in the morning, and you had to be there. If it came onto someone else's patch you'd ask them: "Can I have a shift off you?" and you'd work out the coal that was there together.

'You'd hand-pick the big lumps. The coal was graded into "black diamonds", "cobbles" which were round bits and you got lots of money for those, and "dross" which was more like sand. There'd be a hundred horse and carts at work doing it. Coal salvaging there went on into the 1980s, in fact our youngest daughter Gina used to help us.'

Margaret showed me a photo in an album of Gina in the canteen (*left*) which had been provided for salvagers. Then she picked up another album, which turned out to be full of papers – and there was an odd story to these. A few years ago she had had a motor accident which had left her very depressed. To take her out of herself, Terry and she had gone to live on the estate where Gina was employed to look after racehorses. They lived in a waggon, but one day Margaret discovered an old cottage in the grounds, completely buried in the ground. She and Terry dug it out and began to live in it; Gina's boss charged them one penny a week rent. It was in a very quiet location, far from any roads, it had no main services nearby and not even the postman called. It was at this period in Margaret's life that a strange thing happened, which she outlined thus: 'I was never a scholar, but I began to write stories and poems, they just came to me very easily. This lasted until one day Terry's mum said she wanted us to come back here to live. By an odd coincidence she'd known the old man who'd lived in the cottage. So we came back.' She handed me the file and I read some of her poems and scanned the stories, which were good.

Despite the afternoon having gone on, Gina and her children were still at the trailer. The children were playing outside in what had been a Victorian horse-drawn laundry cart, very tall with big back doors. We went to join them. The children moved to a flat-bedded cart and I photographed Terry and Margaret with them. Then, feeling guilty at having spent so long with them, and after warm goodbyes, I hurried back to my original hosts. That evening Warren and Ada took me out in their car to visit a friend who restored and painted gypsy waggons, but unfortunately he wasn't in. I wasn't too disappointed, however, as I'd had an altogether fascinating day.

I had promised Warren that I would photograph his pride and joy, a coloured yearling horse called Prince, so next morning I went back to do this. Prince was brought down from his field by Sanchaz, who has a true Romany skill with horses. Warren told me proudly: 'Our Sancho can train and break horses, and has driven them on the road since he was five. From August until the fortnight before Appleby, which is in early June, he drove four-and-a-half thousand miles. He even collects rags and delivers coal with a horse and cart.'

I took the photo, and as Sanchaz led Prince away, I felt glad that the Coulsons of Craghead would probably be carrying on their hard-won business for many years to come.

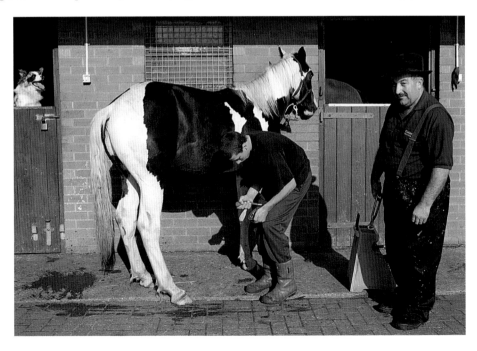

THE CHURCH IN THE WOOD
Family Histories and Hop-picking

In a wood at Bramdean in Hampshire, quite hidden from passers-by, is a small church. It is constructed of corrugated iron painted green, and wood painted white. Cockle shells laid beneath the entrance gate stud out '1883', the date it was built. There is written evidence that 'contractors' were paid for the five weeks' work it took to build the church, but who's to gainsay local lore that gypsies also helped to build it, especially as they always camped nearby on Bramdean Common. Whatever the truth is, the place has become known as the 'Gypsy Church' or the 'Church in the Wood'. The last name comes from psalm 132, verse VI which is:

Lo, we heard it at Ephratah: we found it in the fields of the wood.

These words are engraved on the church's brass candlesticks. For safety, the candlesticks, the harmonium and the movable font are taken out of the church each winter. The Reverend Croad, who like most vicars today looks after several parish churches, opens the Church in the Wood for service only during the summer months – and very pleasant it must be for worshippers to visit the dappled glade.

In the early summer of last year a young couple from Bordon, Kerry and Kathleen Hawkins, took their three youngest children James, Freda Belle and baby Reuben to be baptised at the church. Their eldest son Sam and members of both sides of the family made up the congregation. Kerry Hawkins had asked for his children to be christened at the church because he knew of its gypsy connection. He has gypsy ancestry and is proud of it, and

The christening of Kerry Hawkins' children, James, Freda Belle and Reuben (opposite) Reverend Croad on the steps of the Church in the Wood

Kathleen is pure-bred gypsy; moreover her father Teddy Black had known the Gypsy Church, and so the children's christenings were arranged to coincide as closely as was possible with Teddy's birthday.

This dovetailing of past and present is typical of Kerry and Kathleen. They both have a great interest in their gypsy family history, but Kerry in particular, and he believes there is some truth in the saying: 'The way forward is through the past'! Recently he and

Billie Ayres, Kerry Hawkins' great-great-great uncle hawking goods to the troops
(right) Kathleen's grannie Caroline Smith (right) and her sister in law Alice Ayres (neé Smith). Caroline was a "true"
woman, meaning everything she said came true. A much respected woman, she died in 1967

Kathleen each applied for a pedlar's licence so that he could sell, door-to-door, logs, horse manure and scrap, and Kathleen hand-made flowers, strawberries and haberdashery. In fact the local police had to scratch their heads and consider where the application forms were, since a request for a pedlar's licence is something of a rarity nowadays. Once the forms were located, they found that it was necessary for an applicant to be resident in one location for twelve months, and a short description of what they looked like had to be written down; the sum of £12 25p was required per licence for the year.

When Kerry and Kathleen go hawking they will truly be following in their families' footsteps, for they both come from troop-hawking families. When I met Kerry at their house in Bordon he told me about troop-hawking: 'My grannie's family, the Ayres, would follow the troops on manoeuvres, and when the soldiers fell out for a rest, they would go up to them and sell them sweets, chocolates and fruit. Grannie ran behind the line of soldiers as soon as she could walk. After the Boer War, when the troops came to Bordon, Grannie's family followed them. Kathleen's family, the Smiths, used to troop-hawk in Aldershot, Brighton and Chichester.

'During World War II there was good custom to be had amongst Canadian soldiers. Unfortunately here at Bordon a lot of them got what the gypsies called "the pox" – it might have been yellow fever – and quite a number died. The gypsies got the blame for spreading the disease, and the military authorities had their hawking baskets taken off them and the contents tested – but nothing was found amiss. The gypsies maintained the soldiers caught the epidemic from the lubnis [whores] in London.'

Kerry's abiding interest in the past has led him to collect a good number of old photos, certificates and papers relating to his own and to Kathleen's family. He says it hasn't been an easy task, for being travellers, their ancestors kept on the move and it was only through looking at registers of places where there was seasonal work or fairs that he began to discover material. However, he admits ruefully that a lot of relatives still remain elusive. Old local newspapers occasionally came up with interesting stories. For example in the 21 November 1891 edition of the *Surrey Advertiser and County Times* he found an account of the funeral of his great-great-great-grandfather Paul Ayres, in which the procession was described and the handsome coffin. It also said that despite Mr Ayres having died in Farnham workhouse he was a 'gypsy king' who had 'ample means'. 'My kids were thrilled when I told them they were descended from a gypsy king,' Kerry said, grinning. 'Then I found that the following week's paper had a notice saying that William Ayres, son of Paul Ayres, had been convicted for being drunk and disorderly on the same day that the will had been read; I suppose he was celebrating his legacy!'

Kerry told me that love of the bottle was a failing of Sam Ayres, his great-great-grandfather. Sam also had scant regard for authority, and frequently got into trouble for hawking to troops without the correct papers from the military. Again, local papers reported this. His family have told Kerry what they remember of Sam: for example, 'My gran's cousin told me that when they were all living at the gypsy camp called Hollywater which is near here, a chap hit Sam's younger brother. Sam jumped into his pony cart and drove non-stop the forty miles to Salisbury Plain to challenge the mush to a fight.

'Sam was a rough man, even towards his family. If he came home and found that his wife and kids were having their meal before him, he'd climb up onto the roof of the waggon and put a turf onto the chimney top and smoke 'em out. A lot of the Ayres were tough fighters. Great-gran Ayres' uncles and cousins were feared by other travellers who knew they'd stand no messing. Great-grannie was called Mary Anne. She was at Hollywater Camp when my great-granfer first met her. He was William Othen and his family were steam-engine drivers,

they came to stay in a house just round the corner from the gypsy camp. He married Mary Anne, and his brother married her sister Lena.'

As Kathleen was busy feeding the older children and then putting the baby to bed, Kerry told me about her background. 'Kathleen's grannie who went troop-hawkin' was called Caroline. She was the daughter of Betsy, who had been a daughter of Ben and Betsy Mitchell. Kath's great-great-granfer Ben had the nickname "Rush'n Ben"; family legend

Betsy Ray, daughter of Rush'n Ben

says he got it either through rushing in when he fought, or rushing to take toffs as paying customers to the races! His profession was travelling chimney sweep, and it's said that after he'd committed a serious offence he escaped detection through being unrecognisable at the time because he was covered in black soot! He died in 1906 when he was seventy-seven after being kicked by a horse. His daughter Betsy married James Ray, and one of their daughters was Caroline, Kathleen's grannie.

'As a troop-hawker Caroline struck lucky, for one of the commanding officers took a shine to her and *ordered* his men to buy her goods. She was a quick-witted woman; once when she was stopped by police because she didn't have a "slang" [licence] she argued that because the flowers she'd been carrying were made from all natural materials, that is hazel and berry juice, she didn't need a licence. And through some loophole in the law she couldn't be charged!

'Caroline married Leonard Smith, a "kipsi do-ser" [basket-maker]. He was born in 1900, and on his birth certificate it says that his father Sidney was a "hawker of brushes and mats". The baskets he made were called "spleed", which is a thin strip of wood. He'd shave the bark from a thickish hazel sucker, then when it was still on his knee, he'd nick it with his peg knife. Then he'd take the nicked wood between his thumb and finger, and run it through his teeth to thin it down for weaving. Kathleen's mum told me that sometimes he also used a small metal blade made from a biscuit tin to help split the hazel. He was unusual in using his teeth for thinning, because most travellers worked the hazel on their knee by shaving it thin with a peg knife, then turning it over and starting on the other side.

Leonard Smith

'Leonard also made bee skeps, kneeling mats and pegs. He used to wrap spleed round clothes pegs to secure them, but he banded the straw of his skeps with twine he made from brambles. He made the twine by splitting a bramble through the middle, longways, then scraping out the pith leaving the outside skin. Kathleen's Uncle Dan, Leonard's son-in-law, told me he thinks that the skins were then soaked in water and hung over a rack to dry.'

Kerry then suggested that I ought to meet Uncle Dan, as he could tell me more about Kathleen's grandfather Leonard Smith. Apparently, although Dan's father had been a gamekeeper and churchwarden at East Worldham, there was gypsy blood in the family. Up until the middle of last century Dan's family surname had been Lakey, but they had been caught

Magic lantern slide of basket making

sheep rustling and to throw the police off their trail had changed it to Ham!

Dan Ham was a quietly spoken, easy-going man, still saddened by the death of his wife Janey, sister to Kathleen's mum. He had known her since he was a youth, and they had married in the war years when they were both nineteen. At first Leonard Smith wouldn't give permission for the marriage, and Dan told me how he got round this: 'I got him to sign a paper which I said was to get an extra sugar ration, but it was a wedding consent form, and we got rommer'd [married] at Alton. None of the family came to the wedding, and because we needed witnesses I went out onto the pavement and asked two ladies eating fish and chips if they'd come and witness. At first they said they had to get back to their husbands' dinners, but then they said they would.'

Dan became quickly integrated into gypsy life with Janey, and their first two sons were born in tents. Later he and Janey had a horse-drawn waggon. Dan told me more about his father-in-law: 'He'd buy a field of greens or swedes from a farmer, and they'd bag up as many as they could into a bag. When they got home they'd re-bag them, putting in less so there were more bags, and then sell by the bag. You didn't have to say what weight, you just sold "a bag".

'I'd watch him basket-making. He used a lot of willow besides hazel and stacked it like a big wigwam to dry. His wife went out selling the baskets. Years later when I was doing some tree work at a house I saw one in the porch. I knew it was one of his, and I said to the owners, "Did you buy it off a tall dark lady called Mrs Smith?" – and they had.'

Dan never made baskets himself, but through watching when he was sixteen or seventeen, he learnt from Leonard how to make flowerheads from sticks of hazel or elder. When his future father-in-law was away from the camp, Dan would practise on sticks put ready, and on his return Leonard would be annoyed to find the sticks cut up. However, practice makes perfect, and flower-making from wood is still a skill that Dan has; what is more, he

offered to demonstrate it for me. Kerry and his boys went to get some hazel sticks, and Kathleen took Dan home to pick up his knife. It was one he'd made from a bit of ash with a hole burnt out to take the blade, a blue steel one from an old dinner knife with its tip curved like a parrot's bill. 'The curve helps curl the petals,' he explained. Dan also brought a whetstone, and dampening it with spittle, sharpened his knife against it in a circular motion: 'The art is to get a round edge and to get the right stick. Sometimes you can make a dozen before you get 'em right. You can put a plaster between your finger and thumb if you're doing a lot, as it stops them getting sore, and…' – here he folded a silk scarf – '…you can stop your trousers being rubbed by tying a scarf round your knee.'

He stripped the bark of a hazel stick and placed the stick against his knee, then keeping his knife still but drawing the stick up and down against the blade, scraped down thin strips of wood which began to curl into a ball at the end of the stick. Gradually the ball began to take the shape of a chrysanthemum head. He explained: 'You've got to feel like doing this, to be in the mood, and you need a low seat so your knee's up level.' His knife was making a rhythmic sound as he drew the wood up and down. 'You can hear the knife going well, seems homely to make 'em, some just goes, no trouble. You'd made six or seven dozen a night, that's one every two minutes if it's going right.'

When the head was the size of a good chrysanthemum bloom, Dan cut it off from the end of the stick about half an inch below the 'petals'; then with a short skewer he bored a hole in that end. 'That's so you can push a piece of privet into it, to make the stem. When we were hard up we'd made "quickies", but ones we wanted to look special we'd put into pots – say, a 4in pot which we'd fill first with a layer of moss, then soil half-way up to give it ballast, then fresh green moss on top of that and stick the stems of four or five flowers into that.'

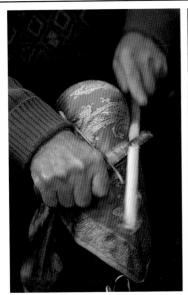

DAN HAM SHOWS HOW TO MAKE WOODEN CHYSANTHEMUMS

Dan ties a silk scarf round his knee to protect his trousers and then starts to peel down thin layers of the stick. It is the stick which is moved not the knife. He pauses from time to time to keep the knife really sharp. The layers are built up until the flower head is complete then a hole is bored into one end of the stick, below the flower head, so that the stem can be inserted.

The finished flower heads are dyed in water in which crêpe paper has been boiled, the colour depending on the flower colour required and then mounted on evergreen stems, such as box, and pushed into a pot part-filled with soil, as ballast, and topped with fresh moss.

However, before being potted Dan's demonstration flowerheads had to be dyed, for they were still natural wood colour. Under Dan's guidance, Kathleen boiled up some crêpe paper so that the dye from it would leach into the water. The children chose bright red crêpe for that purpose. They were enjoying themselves, rolling around Dan's chair and trying to copy him with their own bits of hazel stick. Kerry was having a go, too, and making some impressive specimens which for some reason were curlier than Dan's. Dan quickly dipped each head into the red liquid now in Kathleen's saucepan. 'The curls straighten when you dip them, but as they dry they curl up again,' he said, laying out a row of perfect scarlet chrysanthemum heads. He added, 'We used to make wax flowers, too, on branchy bits of hazel, making the petals from coloured candlewax.'

Kathleen took some unused crêpe paper out of the packet and started to make roses out of it. First she folded the paper, then scalloped the top with scissors. Next she opened the piece out and laid a warm knife against each 'peak' of the scalloping, and curled it into a petal. Lastly she bunched the 'petals' against each other so the whole looked like a rose. To finish off, a piece of thin wire secured with cotton was stuck into a privet 'stem'. Kathleen hadn't made many before, and Dan tried to help; however, he considered crêpe flower-making was 'woman's work' and it was therefore not something he'd done before. Nevertheless the end result was impressive. Kathleen observed, 'They look even better when they're dipped in candlewax, and that helps to protect them when they're hawked round the doors.' Her mother Freda is an expert crêpe flower-maker, but unfortunately she was too busy for me to meet her.

Kerry said of his mother-in-law that she would sell anything and make an offer for anything, it was part of her make-up. He added 'There's a traveller's phrase: "He'd/she'd have a chop [deal] for a walking stick" – and that could have been said about my great-granfer Othen, too!'

I also learned that Kathleen's late father Teddy Black had another well-known gypsy trait: self-sufficiency, and it brought him official recognition, albeit briefly. During the war he was in the Royal Berkshires, and on one occasion a superior officer saw that he'd made a comfortable bender tent and was roasting himself a chicken that he'd 'found' for breakfast. The officer was so impressed he made Teddy into a field corporal – though because he couldn't read or write he had to be demoted.

Dan Ham (aged seventy-five) remembers:

'My mother-in-law cured a lady once with bog alder cockles. The little brown bits the size of your nail. This lady was going to do away with herself because she was so miserable. She had a boil, a carbuncle in a delicate place. You boil the cockles like tea in a kettle or saucepan, strain the liquid out through muslin into a jug and bottle it. It looks like strong tea.'

HOP-PICKING

Kathleen's family had travelled until the 1950s, then they'd all bought plots of ground onto which they settled their trailer. From then on they only moved for hop-picking.

This September work had an essence of its own in the gypsies' yearly calendar, being one of the few times when large numbers of them stayed stationary and in close proximity to each other for several weeks on end. It could be convivial, with socialising and story-telling around camp firesides; but just as easily great rumpuses might erupt, when individual fights became free-for-alls or old feuds were re-opened.

Hop-picking in 1874. The illustration appeared in the 1919 title English Hops *written by George Clinch*

The counties most noted for their prolific hop acreage and thus needing most pickers were Kent, Herefordshire, Worcestershire, Surrey, Sussex and Hampshire. In the latter it was in the eastern part of the county that hops were grown, and this included East Worldham where Kathleen's Uncle Dan had lived. He recalls that as a boy he was paid tuppence a bushel for hops picked, although the price depended on the size of the hop – if they were 'king', that is big, you didn't have to pick as many to make a bushel as you did 'bowsie', or small ones. Dan had met his wife Janey for the first time when the Smiths' waggon had pulled in for the hop-picking. It wasn't unusual for alliances to be formed during this time, and Dan told me the custom was, that if a fellow was interested in a girl he'd throw down his dicklo (scarf) in front of her; it was unlucky to *give* it. If she picked it up and wore it like a headscarf it meant she liked the man.

Selborne, south of East Worldham, was an area where hops had long been grown. Clergyman and naturalist Gilbert White in his book *The Natural History of Selborne*, first published in 1789, wrote of a kind of 'white land' on the north-east of the village which produced the 'brightest hops'. He mentions gangs of gypsy pickers, particularly a well-known family, the Stanleys. The book also includes a letter he wrote to the Honourable Daines Barrington in 1775, in which he comments on the gypsies' ability to withstand severe weather. Part of it read:

> *Last September was as wet a month as ever was known; and yet during those deluges did a young gypsy-girl lie-in in the midst of one of our hop-gardens, on the cold ground, with nothing over her but a piece of blanket extended on a few hazel-rods bent hoop-fashion, and stuck into the earth at each end, in circumstances too trying for a cow in the same condition; yet within this garden there was a large hop-kiln, into the chambers of which she might have retired, had she thought shelter an object worthy of her attention.*

The hop gardens in Selborne belonged to the Earl of Selborne. In 1894 they covered 15 acres (6 hectares) but the present earl recalls that at the peak of the estate's hop-growing days they had 80 acres (32 hectares). A past president of the Hop Marketing Board, and with a great interest in hops and their history, Lord Selborne also told me: 'You'll see a lot of woodland around Selborne, particularly hazel, because it was grown as an undercrop in the woodland and harvested for hop poles.

'The old method of growing hops was to train them up a pole, and then "pole-pullers" cut the hop bine near the ground, pulled the poles up and took them covered in the bine to the hop-pickers. Growing on wires was introduced in about 1900, and then the hop bins were moved along the hops and the top string was cut and the bine pulled down over the bin so that the hops could be stripped quickly into the bin.

'The date hop-picking started never altered by more than a week, so pickers might arrive at the end of August or in the first week of September; the date only become critical when machines came in because they had to be fed with so many bines a minute. We'd have about two hundred gypsy families pull onto the place, and there was a field put aside for them. Men from the estate used to go round and drop off timber each morning for their campfires, and I think they were allowed to take straw from the barn for mattresses. They collected water from the Lion's Mouth, a fountain in the village with an iron lion's head; the water in it comes from a natural spring.

'Hop-picking lasted for three weeks, and during that time the headkeeper on the estate used to keep an eye on the campfires to see if they were roasting pheasants or hares caught by their lurchers. He'd go demented if they were. There was a certain amount of tension between them, and the keepers used to stay up all night during the three-week period.

'My grandfather was president of the Church Army, an off-shoot of the Church of England. It provided an infra-structure for the pickers, and there was a permanent hut here which was their accommodation; in it they held services and helped arrange marriages and baptisms amongst the gypsies.'

I was to hear more about this aspect of hop-picking life from Kerry and Kathleen's families. But first Kerry told me about his mother's father Bert Walker who'd been a pole-puller in the hop gardens. Bert had been a kindly man, and each morning took the bundles of wood left for the campfires and made up the fires with it for the families to sit round – he even filled their kettles and put them on! Kerry joked that being tall, his family did jobs like pole-pulling, but that Kathleen's family, being on the small side, picked the hops when they were down. In fact this wasn't strictly true, for Kathleen's father Teddy Black wore stilts and helped to train the bines up.

The hops had to be picked cleanly from the bine, and if anyone just ran their fingers down and pulled off leaves as well they were barred from the field. 'But there was a saying amongst the pickers' Kerry said 'that to do this the working man was cheating himself.' I was told that the cleanest hop-pickers used to be a big family called Barnett.

Freda, Kathleen's mum, also gave some information about cleanliness, but of a different kind: apparently Lord Selborne used to tell her parents, Leonard and Caroline Smith, to pull their waggon up in the field behind the Lion's Mouth fountain; this was because he knew they were spotlessly clean, unlike the travellers who had come from the Hollywater camp and who were put into a field over the road.

Kerry remembered his granfer Walker telling him about a gypsy called Nelson Marney, the leader of the Marney tribe. Apparently one night Nelson had a row in the Selborne Arms and threatened to fight his opponent in the 'marn-in' and make his eyes like 'saw-cers'; and despite being seventy at the time, he was up at the crack of dawn to renew the challenge. According to Kerry's mum Sheila, each year, regular as clockwork, a big fight would start amongst the travellers. She remembered that one night when she was little there was a fight between the Green, the Stanley and the Ray families, and one of the Stanleys, trying to escape the violence, drove his lorry off with no lights on, narrowly missing the tent that she and some other children were in. The lorry ended up in a ditch, and they were kept awake all night by trouble flaring up all over the site. Freda added that her elder sister Elsie had married a Stanley, Billy, whom she had met whilst hop-picking at Selborne.

On a more peaceful note, Sheila remembered her mother telling her that the vicar had come round the tents asking if any children wanted to be baptised; he also advised her parents to have her christened. She and four other children from the hop-pickers' camp were therefore baptised in the 'big church' at Selborne on the same day, 29 September 1945. Frank Johnson and Carrie Matthews were godparents to them all; one of the Matthews' family had been a daughter of Rush'n Ben and Betsy Mitchell.

I expect if hand-picking hops hadn't finished with their parents' generation, Kerry and Kathleen might have considered a hop-picking baptism for their own children. However, the Church in the Wood at Bramdean was an appropriate and charming alternative, and as Kerry says, 'It made it an occasion the chavvies would remember, like my mum remembers Selborne.'

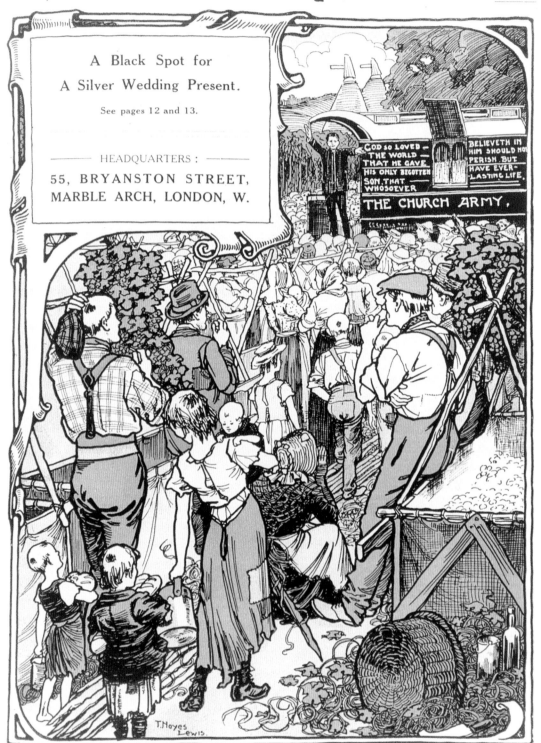

A Black Spot for
A Silver Wedding Present.

See pages 12 and 13.

—— HEADQUARTERS : ——

55, BRYANSTON STREET,
MARBLE ARCH, LONDON, W.

GOD SO LOVED —
THE WORLD
THAT HE GAVE
HIS ONLY BEGOTTEN
SON, THAT
WHOSOEVER

BELIEVETH IN
HIM SHOULD NOT
PERISH, BUT
HAVE EVER-
LASTING LIFE.

THE CHURCH ARMY.

T. Noyes Lewis.

PRICE TWOPENCE.

HOW RELIGION WAS BROUGHT TO HAMPSHIRE HOP GARDENS

Victorian clergyman Samuel Chinn had no romantic illusions about gypsies. He wrote of them: 'Filth and tatters predominate, the men's faces are dark and forbidding, the women seem weather-beaten and miserable, the tents in which they huddle are small and gloomy; in fact, only the young girls with brilliant dark eyes and tawny skin 'the vellum of the pedigree they claim' awaken any romantic and sentimental ideas.

There was one other characteristic of gypsies which concerned him: their nomadic life. As a man of the cloth (he was pastor of the Alton congregational villages churches) he found them well nigh beyond the reach of Christian influence and teaching, for they would be 'here today and gone tomorrow'. This being so, he viewed hop picking as a golden opportunity to take the word of God to them, for it was the one time that they congregated together and remained on one spot for several weeks. Not only gypsies, but tramps too: it was these two categories, together with local villagers, which made up the ten thousand 'hoppers' employed around the Alton district each year.

So it was that in 1861 the Reverend Chinn and his wife began to visit the hop-pickers in the hop gardens, taking religious tracts, bibles and good words. Sometimes they used to attract the attention of the pickers by singing until a group gathered round; or they would go up to the bins where the picking was being done and, as they spoke, pick hops themselves. However, the 'wandering folk of the highways and hedges', as Mr Chinn called them, were not easily won. Some typical responses to the couple were: 'What 'ud I do wi' a tract? Gi'e us a bit of bread and baccy; that's more in our line'; or 'It's hard 'nuff for us folks 'athout troubling our 'eads 'bout 'ligion.' And from one cunning old gypsy woman to the Reverend: 'I should like to marry you, 'cause then I'd have as many glasses [of beer] as I wanted to, and plenty of baccy.' Lesser mortals might have faltered in their cause, but the Reverend and Mrs Chinn carried on and won respect and acceptance and no doubt souls.

Thirteen years after they'd begun their hop-pickers' mission on an evening in 1875, Mr Chinn passed through a large encampment near Binstead. As usual he saw people hanging about aimlessly, others quarrelling or gambling, and so many around the public house that they looked like swarms of bees. He later wrote of that time: 'I was led to consider afresh whether no means could be found whereby they could be more effectively and collectively got at, and especially how something better than the public house could be provided for them to pass the evenings at.'

Rev Chinn's marquee at Binstead

The idea he came up with was to erect a big tent for them to gather in each evening. At first local people were against this proposal because they were fearful of a large group of 'wild and lawless' off-duty hop-pickers. But undeterred, the Reverend Chinn pressed ahead with his plan and rented a marquee which he had erected at Binstead. His plan was to attract pickers to come to it by offering free hot tea from five o'clock (knocking-off time in the hop gardens) until 7pm. Thereafter, hopefully continuing to enjoy the warm and congenial atmosphere, the pickers would stay on in the tent, and the evening would proceed with hymn singing, readings, addresses and magic lantern shows.

The tent duly opened, and a contemporary account calling it the 'Hop-pickers' Mission-tent and Restaurant at Alton' described it as 'spacious' and 'fitted up with seats, platform, harmonium, lamps, texts of scripture, and temperance wallpapers, altogether forming a very pretty appearance and seating three hundred people.'

The first evening was a success. Hoppers turned up carrying, *inter alia*, jampots, saucepans, cracked teapots, old kettles, lids and meat tins in which to receive their free tea.

Magic lantern slide depicting the perils of drink!

Food was not provided, but they were encouraged to bring their own to have with their tea. Moreover the success continued, and every night hoppers crowded to the tent. A city missionary came to take sole charge of preparing the tea and organising the evening programme. Of the evening events, music and singing of Mr Sankey's hymns proved popular, but the most talked about in the hop gardens the next day were the 'dissolving views' or magic lantern slides. These were projected onto a large white sheet and showed, amongst others, 'The Drunkard's Downward Progress to Ruin, Degradation, and Death'; 'The Pilgrim's Progress to the Celestial City'; 'Little Eva' of *Uncle Tom's Cabin* fame; 'The Lost Lamb' (illustrating the parable of the Good Shepherd and his sheep), and a slide of a fat sleek donkey, put in to teach kindness to animals.

The slides which generated most excitement, however, were a set of the gypsies themselves which Mr Chinn had taken. 'Why, there be I, and babby at my breast; and there be ould Granfer!' one woman shrieked in amazement. It was in this section that Mr Chinn had a slide which showed the utterly miserable conditions in which most hoppers lived; this was obviously intended to elicit charitable help when he gave illustrated talks to local dignitaries and townsfolk. But when it was shown to the gypsies themselves their response was not quite as he might have anticipated: 'There they be in the hutch! Eh, now, how comfa'ble they do look.'

The Mission-tent soon proved itself a useful place in which to teach hymns to the hoppers' children. They were knowing little creatures, but the evangelists got the measure of them and made them quiet as mice by wondering out loud what to do with a halfpenny, and then deciding to give it to the first child who learned a hymn by heart. The money was well spent because, of course, the following day the children could be heard singing the hymns all over the hop gardens, and this encouraged their families to visit the tent.

Heartened by the success of the tent at Binstead, the Chinns opened one at Selborne, too, and after that one at Worldham. The average weekly attendances and tea consumption at each were:

Attendance	Binstead: 1,550	Selborne: 1,200	Worldham: 500
Tea drunk	200 gallons	170 gallons	130 gallons

The largest tent was looked after by a congregational minister who spent his holidays 'missioning'. The other tents each had a missionary and young assistant, also working in their vacations; the missionary generally lived in a shepherd's hut loaned by a local farmer. During the day they worked in their pairs, and walked miles carrying

HYMN.

The heathen perish; day by day
Thousands on thousands pass away!
O Christians, to their rescue fly:
Preach Jesus to them ere they die.

Wealth, labour, talents, freely give;
Yea, life itself, that they may live.
What hath your Saviour done for you?
And what for Him will you not do?

Thou Spirit of the Lord, go forth:
Call in the south, wake up the north;
Of every clime, from sun to sun,
Gather God's children into one.

MONTGOMERY.

satchels full of illustrated tracts, gospel books and papers to distribute to the hoppers. Eventually the hop gardens at Bentley, Holybourne and Wyke also had mission tents, making six in all.

The Alton hop-pickers' mission went on for many years under Mr Chinn's supervision; its trials were numerous, but so were its successes. Mr Chinn in his fascinating and now rare book *Amongst the Hop-Pickers*, published in 1887, recorded some of the successes; amongst them the following are perhaps most memorable:

One year, pickers presented him with a banner: 'To Mr Chine, the Hop-picker's Friend, God Loves All.' Touchingly, after the presentation they said, 'You may have the banner, sir, but give us the pole, it's the farmer's, and give us the nails; we had to take them out of our boots to fix it on.'

Then there was the dying man in a London hospital who directed that all his fortune – *viz.* his bible, hymn book and one penny – be sent to John Farley, the missionary for many years at the Holybourne tent, for it was there that he had been converted to Christianity.

On another occasion Mr Chinn met a gypsy on Southsea Common who told him that the bible he'd been given twenty years earlier in the hop gardens had converted his father, his mother and the whole family.

In addition to making conversions, the Mission also succeeded during the hop-picking weeks in getting many pickers to sign the teetotaller's pledge. In fact there was an overall decline in drunkenness, so much so that a special force of constables which had previously always been brought into the Alton area during hop-picking time, was no longer

(*above and right*) *Illustrations by Phiz of hop pickers on the road and resting along the way*

needed. This happy state of affairs was confirmed by the chairman of the magistrates writing to tell Mr Chinn of the 'great improvement in crimes of violence and in drunkenness', and how, in latter years, scarcely a hop-picker had come before the bench.

There were improvements for the hop-pickers, too, because the mission work drew attention to the miserable condition under hedgerows in which most of them slept and cooked. Many farmers, their consciences stirred and no doubt encouraged by their wives and daughters who helped serve tea in the mission tents, agreed to erect wooden barrack-type accommodation for the pickers, and to provide clean straw as bedding.

Tip passed on by a gypsy to a fellow worker in a hopfield:

'To cure your baby of whooping cough boil a white turnip then mix some brown sugar with its juice and give the baby some on a teaspoon.'
Seventy years on, the 'baby' of the above says that this worked on her and on her twin sister.

How Mr Chinn's good works were carried on in Hampshire and elsewhere

The generation of gypsies who still remember seasonal field-work speak of the Church Army as doing good works, and preaching the gospel in hop and fruit fields around the country.

The Church Army was founded by a dynamo of a man, the Reverend Wilson Carlile. He was a curate at St Mary Abbot's in Kensington, London, and his ministry there was unorthodox, involving street processions, open-air meetings and magic lantern shows. This attracted many people who would otherwise never have dreamt of entering a church; however, local residents began to object to the disruption the motley crowds caused on the streets, and Mr Carlile's vicar was forced to ask him to pursue his style of work elsewhere. And so it was that in 1882 he founded the Church Army. It was aligned to the Anglican Church, and Wilson Carlile saw its role as providing a link between that church and the people. Its core was a troop of ordinary working men trained to carry the gospel to the masses.

At first the Church Army was metropolitan-based, but Carlile, having seen the success of the Church of England's Temperance Society's touring van, decided that if he had similar vans his officers could use them to work in country districts, too. His plan was that a van would be the living quarters of a captain and one or two assistants, and it would carry a stock of books which, along with their other duties, the men could sell and thus support themselves. The officer in charge of a van would always ask permission of the local vicar

The Rev Captain Prior and his helpers on the first Church Army mission van, 1892

before pulling into a parish; and at moving on time he would beg the use of local horses to take the van to the next location.

The first mission van took to the road on the 24 June 1892; it was painted dark green, and had quotes of biblical text painted in light green on its sides, and its initial foray from London was to the Kent fruit fields. Many of the pickers there were gypsies who were intrigued to see this version of their own form of transport. One of the first questions they asked of the crew was, 'How much did it cost?' This resemblance of gypsy transport did occasionally backfire. A van evangelist pulling into a village some time later heard a woman say urgently to her son: 'Johnny, run round at once and lock up the fowl-house; there's a gypsy van coming along.'

Once pulled into a parish, the daily duties of the missionaries were visiting and book-selling, and announcing their services. In the evening, if the weather was fine, they would hold an open-air service around the van; that would be followed by a service in a school room, mission hall or the local church. Magic lantern slides, with perhaps the white sheet for them rigged up between some trees or on a caravan, helped to illustrate their talks and also to attract people. By 1908 the Church Army's journal, *The Review*, was reporting that a gramophone was an even greater draw than magic lantern slides; one was often played in what was known as a 'social tent'. This was a large tent pitched near to the mission van and lit by oil lamps; inside it was a table set with free writing materials – the stamps had to be purchased – and one of the missionaries would be on hand to write a letter if needed. Magazines and papers were also put out for people, and games and concerts were laid on, with music supplied by the gramophone or other sources. At some locations, particularly where there were large gatherings of hop- or fruit-pickers, one of the Army's trained nurses would attend and could be consulted free of charge.

The 'Oxford' Church Army van, 1895

An account written in 1905 puts the number of vans in operation at that time as being sixty-six. Each had to pay an annual hawker's licence fee of £2!

Living conditions within a van were not ideal. The overall floor size was 10ft x 6ft (3 x 1.8m), but once a stove, table and lockers were installed, this was reduced to 6ft long by 2ft wide (1.8 x 0.6m). Across one end were two bunk beds, and a third bed along one wall served as a seat during the day. On cold nights after the stove had gone out, condensation formed on the inside of the half-inch-thick plank walls, and by morning blankets were often frozen to the walls.

> Romani verses collected and translated by Captain L.O.C. Langridge of the Church Army:
>
> *A Romani rai, and a Romani chai*
> *Shall jaw t-sawler and drab the bawler*
> *And dook the grai of the farming rai.*
>
> (*Translation:*
> A Romany man and a Romany girl
> Shall discuss together and poison the pig
> And steal the horse of the farm owner.)
>
> *Can you rokkai Romani? Can you fake a bosh?*
> *Can you kiss a pretty mot underneath the cosh?*
> *A hi didikai – chavi you do know*
> *In the rani, in the sawni, in the pani.*
>
> (*Translation:*
> Do you speak the Romani? Can you mend an umbrella?
> Can you kiss a pretty girl in the wood?
> Oh yes, you half-caste – but the children are watching
> I'll kiss and love my queen when it's dark and we'll collect the water in the morning.)

Not being ordained, van evangelists were not able to perform baptisms or marriages, but they did encourage and arrange both. Baptisms were carried out by the local vicar, who would either visit an encampment or perform the rite in the village church. Marriage ceremonies, and particularly gypsy ones, were usually at a registrar's office. However, having said this, Captain John Smith, the present-day archivist of the Church Army, has an interesting account of a church wedding of gypsies, written by Captain L.O.C. Langridge who arranged the event in 1927.

Captain Langridge was in charge of a mission van which served in the New Forest area; it was called 'Winchester 2'. With a cadet to help him, he travelled between the parishes and the gypsies, spending a fortnight with each in turn. At Colbury they came across two gypsy brothers living with, but not married to,

A double gypsy wedding. The service was taken by Captain Langridge of the Church Army

two gypsy sisters; each couple had children. Captain Langridge tried to persuade them it was right that they should marry, an idea to which the men agreed, but not the women. He writes of what happened next:

'Finally I said "Well! you know where my van is, I'm having a service tonight with your people. If you think any more about it, come and see me!" The service began, and included lantern slides. In the middle of my talk a man sidled up to me and said, "Captain, Mrs wants to see you." I replied, "Well, Mrs will have to wait until the service ends." When I had packed away my lantern gear at the end, they came up into the van with a crowd of relations, and the man said, "We think you were quite right, Captain, and we want to get married."'

Captain Langridge therefore set about making arrangements for a double wedding. The vicar agreed to call the banns and marry them without making a charge; he booked the marriage for New Year's Day 'to start the year well'. Langridge then went to a well-to-do lady who donated enough money for him to buy two wedding rings; another lady supplied dresses; and his sister gave him ladies' hats and shoes. He looked out a suit which would fit one of the grooms, and a friend provided another. A baker gave an iced cake, and an after-wedding meal was arranged at a gypsy's house situated nearby in the forest.

On the wedding day the grooms, plus many relatives, drove up in a ramshackle car with broken springs. Captain Langridge gave them white ribbons for their buttonholes. Once the ceremony was under way, he helped with the responses, and as best man, gave the brides away. Afterwards they all posed for a photograph, and then according to Captain Langridge: 'We clambered into the old car and there was nowhere for me to sit, but at their feet on the floor. After a bumpy ride we arrived at the house for a meal, and they were so excited they couldn't cut the cake and I had to do that for them. Some time afterwards I heard that they were still happily married…'

> **An Old Gypsy Love Charm:**
> Take an onion, a tulip, or any root of the kind (ie a bulbous root) and plant it in a clean pot never used before: and while you plant it, repeat the name of the one whom you love, and every day, morning and evening, say over it:
>
> As this root grows
> And as this blossom blows,
> May her/his heart be
> Turned unto me.
>
> And it will come to pass that every day the one whom you love will be more and more inclined to you, till you get your heart's desire.

One of the last Church Army officers to go to Selborne in Hampshire in 'hopping' time was Captain Gordon Church. He helped to man the Army's mobile cinema van (first used in 1947) which showed religious and educational films; the van had a rear projection screen, and the loudspeakers mounted on the roof were as loud as ghetto-blasters. Reminiscing, Captain Church says: 'The visit to Selborne completed the summer work as far as the "daylight cinema" van was concerned.

The Church Army with the New Forest gypsies, 1914

'As far as I can remember, the Church Army's role to the hop-pickers there was rather different to that in the Kent hop-fields. The Church Army officer ran a sort of medical mission – he lived in a tent, as did the hop-pickers, on the edge of a large circular field, and he used to go round with a medical bag shouting: "Any births, bumps or bruises?" As you can imagine, his ministrations in these matters were very welcome as the kids were always knocking one another about in their play.'

The Church Army's mobile cinema van was eventually ousted by the popularity of television and was shipped off to the Church Army in Australia, and by the late 1960s the Mission vans had dropped out of use altogether. However, the work of the Church Army continues in its many forms, and undoubtedly succeeds in providing that which perhaps all missionaries have always sought (and not forgetting the pioneering Reverend Samuel Chinn): a little heaven on earth.

LIVING WAGGONS

The first old-fashioned gypsy caravan I ever saw stood in the corner of a field, snug behind a high hedge; it belonged to the grannie of my playmates in the 1950s. They lived with their parents in a bender tent next to their grannie's waggon, and just across from both was a modern trailer, bright with chrome, in which their uncle lived. Although I didn't appreciate the fact at the time, these three homes showed at a glance how travellers' accommodation had evolved over the generations.

Until about the middle of the nineteenth century, gypsies lived in bender tents which were carried on pack animals or in covered carts; however, as road surfaces improved and as craftsmen were increasingly available to supply living waggons at a reasonable cost, the 'vardo', as gypsies call it, became their main form of transport and accommodation – though tents continued to be used as well, because often a vardo was too small to house all the family. Then in the 1950s, motor-drawn trailers began to supersede the traditional vardoes.

I remember that my friends' grannie's vardo was painted dark red on the outside, and that inside, the brass handles and knobs on the dark wooden drawers and cupboards shone brightly. I believe it was of the type known as a 'Reading', made popular by a firm called Dunton & Sons of Reading, Berkshire. A 'Reading' waggon had a straight-sided body which sloped inwards slightly from the top and was set between big back wheels. Another waggon named after a place was the 'Burton', after a firm in Burton-on-Trent; this was a heavy type of waggon generally bought by showmen rather than ordinary gypsies. Many other gypsy waggons took their names from their appearance. Thus the 'Ledge' had straight sides downwards from the roof, but approximately three-quarters of the way down, each side tucked under into a right angle, and this narrowed base rested on a ledge over the wheels. A bow-, or barrel-top had a rounded or square canvas top.

Whatever their style, the layout of most gypsy waggons was roughly the same. The door was at the front and was divided horizontally so that the top could be opened in warm weather; there was often a small window, too. A bunk bed was built across the back end of the six-foot square interior, and the space beneath was enclosed by doors; thus during the day, bedding could be stored behind the doors, and at night when this was taken out, the cavity became an additional sleeping-place. Cupboards and shelves were fitted on the side walls, and a stove or grate on the left-hand side near the door; its chimney would be positioned on the right of the roof or near its middle – like this it would avoid damage from overhanging branches when the waggon was travelling along the road.

High quality interior fittings, exterior and interior carving, and gold leaf in the paint-work were all features which characterised the more expensively made waggons. There is a stunning example of this sort at the Hereford and Worcester County Museum at Hartlebury Castle: it is a 'Reading' built in 1919 and reputedly once owned by a gypsy queen. There are gold lion-head gargoyles at each roof corner with lead piping coming from their mouths to spout rainwater. The waggon's body is intricately worked, with many carvings of flowers, grapes and leaves, and a great deal of chamfering to uprights – this last is done not to look decorative, but to lessen the weight of the woodwork. The exterior has a base colour of crimson lake, and there is green, scarlet and a liberal application of gold leaf in the decora-tive paintwork overlaying it.

Inside is a bow-fronted chest-of-drawers; a lit-tle cupboard with a mirror front; an impressive bunk bed with a carved horse's head and whip above it; and a fireplace backed by a blue and white enamel surround. Over the fireplace is a mantelshelf enclosed by burnished steel bars and uprights topped with finials, and above that, mir-rors with decoration cut into them. How proud the gypsy queen must have felt travelling in such style!

Of course, not all vardoes were carved and expensively decorated. Midlands gypsy Les Elliott owns and still travels in a beautifully painted old 'Ledge' and has a highly decorated smaller waggon; but he told me that years ago many gypsies could-n't afford expensive materials, and so painted their waggons simply and cheaply. This is corroborated by a letter written in 1912 by gypsiologist Alice Gillington, in which she bemoans the fact that she hasn't the time to restore the interior of her waggon to its original red, green and blue, for to do so she would have to chip off 'the coat of drab paint' put over it by its previous own-ers, the Bowers family.

Probably the only type of horse-drawn gypsy caravan still being made is the 'open-lot', the style favoured by New Age Travellers. Its green bowed canvas top is brightly visible, and generally there's a coloured horse between the shafts clip-clopping smartly along the road. An open-lot has a bed and wheels from a four-wheeled flat cart, and the canvas top is open at the front (hence the name 'open-lot'); wooden pillars to the left and right of the opening support the roof and provide places on which to screw handles to help you get in and out. Open-lots are often made by gypsies, and generally there are a few for sale at gypsy horse fairs.

Opposite: An elaborately painted bow- or barrel-top waggon and (above) Les and Edna Elliott's open-lot showing the compact layout of the interior

LOL THOMPSON

It was at Appleby Horse Fair that I came across Lol (Lawrence) Thompson selling a couple of open-lots he'd made and decorated. Ironically, Lol was born just at the beginning of the era when the motor trailer was becoming popular, but he knows a great deal about horse-drawn waggons, having been brought up in one. He is a good-looking fellow with regular features – though one of the first things you notice are his tattoos, so prolific he's almost as decorative as his waggons. He has more of them on his left arm than his right because, artist that he is, he's done them himself; in fact has made a unique tattooing machine using the staccato movement of the hammer in an electric doorbell.

When we met, Lol was sitting in one of his open-lots, waiting for prospective customers. His pretty fair-haired wife Toni was in a modern trailer parked next door, and their son Samuel ran between the two. It was early morning and there didn't seem to be many potential waggon purchasers about, and so I asked if he would mind telling me how he came to be a waggon-builder and painter. He rolled himself a cigarette and said he'd be happy to: this is his story:

'When my grandparents died their vardoes were burnt and all their worldly possessions – too many sad memories to keep 'em. But we did hang on to one wagon and lived in it. We camped at South Shields, and from when I was thirteen I helped Dad collect scrap. He'd hire horses and carts from a Gateshead scrapyard for £2 a day; they were rubbishy old carts with neckties for harness, but you could get a day's work with 'em. When we took the load back they'd deduct the £2 from what the load was worth, say we might have £3 of woollens, £1 of rags, 30s worth of aluminium, and such-like.

'When I was about seventeen the price of scrap went up – miners were then earning about £28, but we were getting £60 a week! I'd always wanted my own horse and cart and so I started to save up for them, and eventually bought a brand new rolley – that's a four-wheeled cart, Londoners say trolley. Then I went to an auction and bought a young horse which had been yoked only two or three times.

'I went to work with them, and when I went into gardens to collect, my brother would stand in the road holding the horse's head. We did this for a month to train it, but it wasn't 100 per cent reliable, so when my brother couldn't help and I knew I was going to be leaving the horse for a longish time, I put a four-stone weight on a chain with a hook which I brought between its front legs and hooked onto the bridle. This worked well, and eventually I didn't need the weight because the horse would stand of its own accord.'

Opposite: Lol Thompson in one of his open-lots

Lol stopped here, for a truck had pulled up outside the waggon; the driver wound down the window and held out some gold rings in his palm and asked if Lol wanted to buy one – but he declined. It was the first of several interruptions of the kind; the next was a young gypsy girl, on foot, carrying a roll of net-like material which she was trying to sell at so much a length to caravanners on the site. Lol continued:

'I used to carry an empty milk churn on my rounds which I'd fill with water for the camp just before I went back. One day the horse bolted into a flat-out gallop. I was lying over full-stretch, and the pressure from the reins was lifting the back wheels off the ground. We were heading for a roundabout, then the front wheel hit a curb and the rolley went up in the air, throwing me and the milk churn out onto the road; by the time I'd got up, the horse and rolley had gone. A man in a transit van stopped and I jumped in, but I was in the passenger side and when we caught up to the cart I couldn't get at the horse, so I got out. The horse wasn't half going a speed! It turned into the main road and went by a bus and overtook a bin lorry. There was a police car chasing it by now, and it was white with lather and beginning to tire. Eventually we got it and I calmed it down and took it back home.

'From then on my brother *had* to help me, because once a horse has bolted it'll do it again – and it *did*, it went through a wall and the rolley hit a lamp, the harness snapped and the rolley wheels were all broken and bent.

'I sold the horse to Lynemouth in Northumberland to haul sea coal, very hard work, more stone than coal, and I had to borrow a horse and cart again. Of course I had the smashed-up rolley and I got a joiner to repair it, but I found that half my wages were going to him every week in payment so to cut down on cost I decided to paint it myself. I got two tins of paint, one white, one yellow and mixed them, experimenting to get the right colour for the wheels – and I got it spot on! Then I did the shafts and other bits, and filled in the narrow strips of chamfered wood with a kid's paintbrush.

'Not long after a bloke came and asked me if I'd paint the wheels on *his* waggon – and that's how I got started, painting and eventually making my own waggons.'

Lol's wife brought us two cups of tea, and a woman came up to enquire of Lol how much he wanted for the open-lot we were sitting in. He replied '£3,500'. She looked thoughtful, but didn't commit herself. I asked him how many waggons he made a year. 'Two or three. I buy the wood – parana pine, ash and some hardboard. The work takes time – for instance, for chamfering I use a knife and sandpaper, there's no tool can do it.'

'Where do you get the wheels and metal bits?'

'I go from one end of the country to the other looking, and people tell me where they've seen some. It's hard to find springs and turntables, and especially the flat-headed nuts and bolts. I make a lot of those meself.

'Occasionally I paint cars for people. You can paint a motor in a day, but it takes three weeks to paint a waggon top to bottom – and that's provided you're in shelter, because if you're outside you have to wait for the dew to dry. After painting, waggons have to be varnished. This one has been varnished three times, and if I kept it I'd varnish it every year.'

He went on: 'I don't like selling them until I've lived in them, they get weathered then, look used. My wife lives in the modern trailer, but I live in a waggon the year round. Of course I sell to people who just want something ornamental, but I do like to see them used, and I look out for them to see how they've stood up to the winter.'

I commented on the number of horses' heads painted on both the outside and the inside of the waggon. Lol explained that they were his trademark, and he also pointed out that whereas other waggon painters' horses' heads looked the same, every one of his was different. We looked at them, and they were, too – there was even one which had one black ear and one white! Even the copper kettle on the stove had a horse's head engraved on it!

Next, Lol pointed to a piece of metal at the back of the stove, and said, 'When you've been brought up in a waggon you know which bits can catch fire. My dad used to get a piece of scrap tin or use the top of an old spin-drier to keep heat from the back of the stove, but when I make a waggon I get metal and cut out a piece especially for the job. Of course, years ago there was no special painting up, and my mum and dad just used to paint their waggon to make it waterproof – though the rain still came in. It was warm though, and there was always the kettle on and some bacon bones and tatties and turnips boiling. It had a white canvas cover, though you couldn't keep it white, especially after winter when it had got darkened down by soot, so in the spring it was painted white and re-varnished inside.

'Ways of painting are changing, even today. Jim Berry was the one and only, the best waggon painter. He's dead now, but he lived in Doncaster which is a good place because it's central, the south below, the north above and plenty of places to get repairs done to a waggon. But nowadays, his painting, you'd think it plain and drab. You see, the colours and quality of the brushes are better. One time a waggon was only painted in undercoat and you "lined" with gloss, which would stretch, and used gloss for lettering; now, proper sign-writers use enamels.'

Lol's next stop was to be Barnards Castle, which is where travellers usually go after Appleby. Then, he hoped, there would be some steam-engine restoration work going for him in Teesdale.

Dick Harrison

THE HARRISONS OF SKIPTON

Dick Harrison is a retired garage owner of gypsy blood, and he agreed to talk to me about the old days of his family's business in Skipton, North Yorkshire. I duly arrived in Skipton on a mild September afternoon, but with two or three hours to spare. Not liking to bring my appointment forward – Dick is much respected amongst the northern gypsy community, and I held him somewhat in awe – I explored Skipton instead. It was market day, and stalls lined each side of the High Street; they gave the town an 'olde worlde' look, and went well with the pavements which were black rectangular blocks of granite set like cobbles, and in places surrounded by worn York paving. The row of shops and old inns on one side of the road was cut through every so often by a narrow alleyway; these led straight to the canal behind.

Halfway down the other side of the High Street was the town hall, and within it was the Craven Museum; it was open to the public, so I went in. When I asked if they had any gypsy items, it turned out that they did have a couple: a longish rope made completely of black horse hair, and a horse's tail. The rope had been donated in 1965 by Mr Isaac Miller in memory of his father Jacob, and the tail came from the same source and was labelled 'Tail

The Leeds & Liverpool Canal at Skipton

*The horse-hair rope and the tail of the
trotting horse, Cowboy*

of "Cowboy", a trotting horse'. Mr Miller had apparently lived near to the canal; later I was told that he had died and that the family had moved away, although I was to find out this wasn't completely true.

I then drove to the outskirts of Skipton to meet Dick Harrison. His house was set in an interesting area, for the most part industrial, which was obviously good for his garage business, but with the Leeds to Liverpool canal running through fields behind, and way out in front and beyond the built-up area, the hills of the Pennine chain.

Dick came to the door dressed in a beautiful suit and a fine lawn shirt with a silk stripe in it. He later told me he's always worn a suit for his work, even as a youth. On one of his fingers he wore an eye-catching diamond ring, the stones set three across in traditional gypsy fashion.

There was much to hear about and – I was to find out – to see, so we wasted no time in starting to talk about Dick's life in and around Skipton. As he told me: 'My mother's father, Richard Burnside, was a horse dealer, and he married a girl called Mary Firth from Thorne; at the time they were both travellers. Then they stopped travelling and settled in Skipton. My father's parents came from Skerton in Lancashire. Dad had spent some time in the Isle of Man, driving a landau, cabbing, and he did the same in Morecambe. He served in the Great War in the trenches and got shrapnel wounds, he was gassed, and he got malaria, too – but he never talked about it. He didn't come to live in Skipton till after he was married.

'He probably met my mother at Appleby or at Brough Hill Horse Fair. My mother always told me that Appleby and Brough Hill started when the English were fighting the Scots, and dealers used to take horses there for the military because they were the nearest places to the fighting.

'Father used to horse deal and buy scrap. He drove a pot cart made by Abe Ashton of Preston – they were called pot carts because years ago gypsies used them to carry earthenware from the potteries which they'd travel with and sell as they went. In later years me brother broke the pot cart up. You see, it was in his yard never being used, and he'd have to keep moving it from one part to another so that he could store scrap, and he got fed up with doing this so broke it up. Dad went mad.

'My mother used to hawk sheets and drapery; she did this for years, going on the bus to different villages. We children – that's myself and my younger brothers Jim and Bill – were brought up to go to Sunday school every week, that was a *must*. And we

Dick as a young boy

(left) Richard Burnside, Dick's grandfather and (above) his wife Mary Firth

(below left) Mary Firth with Richard Burnside
(below right) Dick's father in the WWI uniform of the Lancasters

kept to the custom on Good Friday of never eating meat; also on that day we never knocked in a nail or put in a screw or used a hammer, and sewing wasn't allowed, although you could sell a horse.

'After school I used to hawk loose bananas round the streets, one penny for two. We got them from the market, they were the ones which fell off when the man there cut the stalks. At that time too, I'd walk round the streets and if I saw an old bike in a backyard not being used I'd ask to buy it for 9d or a shilling; then I'd do it up and sell it.

'Father dealt in farm horses, mostly Dales which are about 14.2hh, though the breed has got more like Fells now, which are taller and stronger. He rented fields to put them in, and had stables which I'll show you later.

'Mondays were busy days, meeting and talking to farmers in the cattle market. No point in going round the farms that day because they'd all be in the market.'

I asked Dick how much a horse would have cost in those days. He considered a moment, then replied: 'Well, Father paid £9 for Kitty. He bought her from one of Mother's relatives, Uncle Herbert Hudson. Kitty pulled the cart, but she was hard-mouthed and took a lot of holding. If she had a ton of scrap on you couldn't hold her, for as soon as she turned for home, she was off. She once took eighteen hundredweight of copper and brass into Bradford – a distance of eighteen or nineteen miles and which included going up a big hill – in only one hour and twenty minutes! Father sold her back to Uncle Herbert who lived at Bradford, and he'd take her to Morecambe every summer selling wholesale fruit; used to hawk it. People used to say, "That Kitty, being driven all the way to Morecambe!" – but he'd break the journey by stopping with us at Skipton, and when she was in Morecambe she was there for some time.

'We used to go with our waggon to Appleby Fair every year. We liked to go, looked forward to it, staying on the roadside with stick fires. Going up, Mother would take a big basket and hawk the farms. I was in the waggon with me father. When they got to Appleby all the travellers used to stop on the roadside for the fair, not on a hill as they do now. When I was a kid that hill was full of gorse bushes.'

I asked Dick if he had any old photos, and he got up to look. I'd taken him a pot plant which, after being shut in the car for so many hours, looked as if it needed a

(top) Dick's Mum and Dad; (right) Dick's uncles with their cart, taken in Lancaster

drink. I went to the kitchen sink and poured some water into the pot; a bit of the soil-specked water fell on the draining board, and in mopping it up I dropped some drips into the washing-up bowl. Meanwhile Dick had found the photos and was stood behind me, and remarked that the bowl was strictly for washing up – it was one of their customs. I felt contrite that I'd polluted it, and wished I hadn't been so bold as to water the plant. We talked a little about taboos and cleanliness; Dick said that cats were considered to be dirty, and that he wouldn't even let a dog in the house.

Dick leading Kitty pulling the gala cart at Skipton Gala

We sat down, and he showed me a photo of himself as a youth leading a pony and decorated cart at Skipton Gala. 'The pony is called Kitty, but it's not the same Kitty that Father had from Uncle Herbert. I used to drive this one, and every year take it to the gala and the crowd would throw pennies into the cart. My first job – I never worked for anyone in me life except Father – was going round with that pony and cart buying empty sacks, so much a dozen. I also bought old fat hens for killing from farm sales or from surrounding farms, 9d or a shilling each, then sell them to butchers, who'd sell them for broth-making. If there was snow on the ground I'd leave the cart and catch the bus instead. I'd buy perhaps three or four, put them in the sack and come back on the bus with them.

'I used to keep bantams at home, not for their eggs, but because I liked them. Eggs were never a problem to get, for when we were going round the farms you could get them for very little. I'd use Kitty and the cart to collect wool, too. Before the Wool Marketing Board, Father used to buy whole fleeces, but after it came into being we weren't allowed to buy fleeces; so we bought "doddings", that's scrap bits left over once the fleeces have been sorted out. We'd get a farthing a pound weight commission from the Wool Board. After I married I had a lorry, and I used to go into Scotland and buy a lot of wool and take it to John Hudson's, a big mill at Keighley, and later, when the Wool Marketing Board was operating, to them at Bradford.

'Father and me used to hawk flowers, too, in the spring, especially at Easter time. We'd buy them, mostly daffs, in St James's Market, Bradford, and spend a couple of months with a basket round the streets. In January we sold firewood. And when we weren't selling firewood, flowers or wool, there was the hens and the hoss trade. We used to break horses too; mouth and lunge them and ride 'em, put 'em in and keep 'em going. We bought our corn from A.J. Clayton of Skipton.'

Dick broke off to suggest we go into Skipton so that I could meet his brother Bill and see the family's old stable block which Bill still keeps intact.

In Skipton we turned into a small street not far from the canal. Bill lives in a sturdy stone house (once occupied by a mill manager) at one end, and the stables and the waggon

Granny Mary Firth with her daughters, Dick's aunties and (right) the unusual home-made ladder

house are next along. Not far beyond, at the other end of the street, is the house where their parents had lived and brought them up. Tall new houses surround the little street and make the stables and yard appear very much an oasis of the past.

As we walked to the stables, Dick explained that their grandfather Burnside had built them, and that their father had bought them. Today the two stalls in the stable are used as store-rooms, but iron hay-baskets and harness brackets are still on the walls, as is a ladder ingenious in its simplicity: a thick plank nailed to the wall and punctuated with stirrup-shaped toeholds; it leads up to the hayloft over the stable. The cobbled floor was well swept, and Dick told me that in the yard's heyday the top half of the walls would be kept whitewashed, and the bottom painted with tar which acted as an 'antiseptic'. By putting gates across the bottom of the stalls to make a loosebox they were able to get eight horses into the stable.

It was obvious the place evoked many memories for the brothers. Dick recalled: 'Even when I was going to school, the first thing I had to do every morning, even before having a cup of tea, was look to the horses in here, and it was my last job at night, too. They had to be given water, and be fed and kept clean. There's an old saying: "A good clean is as good as a feed", and we groomed before they went out and at night as well.' I asked if that was just for the horses they had for sale. 'No, even ones we kept had to be groomed, and their harness cleaned, too. The hames were nickle-coated, and so were the harness buckles, and we kept them bright with metal polish.'

'When I was sixteen I got my leg broken in here, and was put on traction. It was my own fault, I'd been out hawkin' flowers and was in a hurry. I rushed in with a bag of grass on my back, we used to get grass from freshly cut tennis courts or scythe some from the roadside, and I frightened the horse. I looked down and my leg was swinging.'

Bill told me that the stable muck went into a heap by a side wall in the yard. 'It was sold for 5s a load delivered. It had to stand twelve months or more because people wouldn't have it if it was any fresher!'

Back at his house Bill produced a box of old photos, and there were several of their grandparents and parents. The ones of their father showed him wearing clogs, and I commented on this; Bill said: 'He always wore them, but me and Dick used to wear Luton boots, they were like a short riding boot with an elastic side, 7s 6d a pair for kids and 12s 6d for grown-ups.'

Dick (right) with his brother Bill outside the old stables

Another photo showed their father, looking advanced in years, by a horse and cart. Dick told me: 'Even when he was eighty he still used to help. Then we went into the motor trade and he couldn't. He died a week before his ninety-fifth birthday.'

Jean Hudson

Seeing my fascination with old photos, Dick said we should go to visit his half-cousin Jean Hudson, because he was sure she would have some. So we left Bill, and went to meet Jean in her immaculate little house on the canal-side. Jean is related to Dick through his mother's side of the family. It is obvious they are a close-knit dynasty, and later, when the subject of marriages came up in conversation, Dick joked, but meant it: 'There's a saying, "Get a cat of your own kind, even if it scratches your eyes out!"'

Prepared beforehand by a phone call, Jean had kindly looked out some photos. Her maiden name had been Miller, and one photo she showed me was of her father James riding his brother Isaac's horse 'Cowboy' to victory at Kilnsey races. 'Cowboy used to pull a cart, but he won this trotting race,' she explained. I said, 'I've seen his tail, it's in the museum and there's a horse-hair rope, too!'

'That's right,' Jean confirmed. 'Uncle Isaac gave them in memory of grandfather Jacob.'

Some of Jean's photos showed Appleby Fair, and one (shown opposite), taken about sixty years ago, showed her as a little girl amongst a large, happy-looking group there.

Jean had an appointment to keep in the town, so Dick suggested we move on to his son Jim's place and talk to Jim's wife Carol Ann because she had some photos of Appleby, too. I was certainly meeting the family!

We drove on through a few streets to a smart-looking yard in which there were piles of fencing material and gates. Supplying these is Jim's busi-

This tattered but much prized photo shows Cowboy being ridden to victory

ness. He is the eldest of Dick's three children; the other two are George and Susan. Jim met us in his office, which is on the ground floor of their new house, built in the middle of the yard. The office is cleverly designed to be part of the business section, and a separate door-way takes visitors to an impressive stairway which leads up to Jim and Carol Ann's living accommodation. Leaving Jim to his work, Dick and I ascended the stairs – and at the top stepped into the most lovely surroundings. I discovered this was Carol Ann's doing; she had designed the house, and no doubt had much to do with choosing the beautiful interior fixtures and furnishings.

When we arrived she willingly stopped what she was doing to go and look for photos. She returned with a bagful, and kneeling on the carpet, petite and attractive, began to rum-

Jean Hudson (second left, front row) holding the hand of her cousin Totty Miller, amongst a group at Appleby Fair

mage through. There were a lot of Appleby, though taken in more recent times. She explained to me that Appleby Fair meant a lot to her, because coming from a traveller family she's known it all her life – in fact, she'd met Dick's son Jim there! She told me how girls were able to meet boys at Appleby Fair time in the 1960s:

'All the teenagers used to go to a dance at Kirkby Thore. Entrance was half-a-crown, and only soft drinks and crisps were sold. Dad used to take me and bring me back. Even when I was able to drive myself there, Mum would be out with a torch waiting for me to come home!'

She went on: 'Years ago there were no trade stalls at the fair, like now, just a man selling blankets and a pot man who displayed his wares on the roof and bonnet of his car – oh, and there was a harness stall. When I first started to go, the fair was held on the roadside, and not on the hill as it is today. In those days you knew who was going to park beside you, say the Millers one side and the Smiths the other, but a few years ago we stopped going for a while because it changed, all sorts used to go there and you didn't know who'd be camping

beside you when you woke up. It's getting better now and we love to go. I take up some food and put it in the fridge in the trailer, and we have a glass of wine with our meal beside the open fire.'

When Carol Ann related how the fair had improved of late I suspected that this was probably due in no small way to Dick, because he is one of the leading members of the committee which runs it. Before we left, Carol Ann found me a photo (right) she particularly liked because it showed four generations of Harrisons: her little son Dick, her husband Jim, his father Dick, and Dick's father Jim!

Jean's aunt Margaret (her mother's sister) and her family

1947 postcard of Appleby Fair

By this time Dick and I were both famished, so we went into an in-store cafeteria. Dick admitted that eating out was still something of a novelty. His wife Hannah May, whom he had loved dearly, had died in 1983, and during all the years of their marriage they had only had about six meals out. He told me proudly: 'She could make a meal out of nothing!' When the waitress came and put our plates of food onto the table Dick looked down at his and said severely, 'I wouldn't give that to my dog!' The waitress looked alarmed. There was a pause, then suddenly he beamed and announced, 'No, I'm going to eat it myself!'

Dick with his relatives

We ate, and talked of Dick's life since he retired from his car sales and garage business. He now has time for his great passion, horse trotting races. He told me: 'I've been interested in it for years, and I've had a sulkie, and trained horses for trotting. Father wouldn't have anything to do with it, he used to say, "A trotter makes a rich man poor and a poor man lousy!" That's because they take up so much time, and you'd neglect your work to take them to the races.

A trotting horse with a sulkie

'There are "pacers" and "trotters", and they're usually in separate races. A "pacer" is a natural gait – like a dog, the back and front leg goes the same on the same side. A trotter's action goes one, two, three, four. I've been all over the world to trotting competitions, and many times to America where trotting horses make big money. I've a photo of myself in America stood next to a horse called Nialator which was sold for twenty million dollars – and there was a horse called MacScooter which made thirty-five million!'

Dick's role as a committee member for Appleby Horse Fair also takes up time – it's probably the biggest horse fair in the world. He explained how the committee for it started: 'It was over thirty years ago when the Catholic priest from Kirby Stephen came and told us that the authorities wanted to do away with the fair, and we had to get together to really fight to keep it. Captain Lonsdale came on the committee. His family had owned the land, and in their castle archives we found James II's charter granting the right to hold the fair, and it needed an act of parliament to stop it. So the fair was saved, although the committee was kept on to run it.'

Listening to Dick talking of Appleby, I remembered how earlier he'd told me of his mother explaining the fair's history to him, and how the family had looked forward to going to it; how his half-cousin Jean had photos of the fair from her childhood, and how Carol Ann loves it too and had met Jim there. With all that, plus Dick's own role in helping to run the fair today, it seemed to me that Appleby and Harrisons are as enduringly woven together as, well… as the strands in the museum's fine horse-hair rope.

TYSSUL & MAGGIE BURTON

Tyssul and Maggie Burton live on the outskirts of a small town not far from Carmarthen. 'Tyssul' is a name I'd never encountered before, and later he was to tell me it came from the Welsh word for 'Sunday': this can be either 'Sul' or 'Dyddsul', and because in the past people dealt with the spoken, rather than the written word, it is likely that over the generations 'Dyddsul' has become adulterated to 'Tyssul'. Another explanation for the name is that it comes from the place Llandysul where there was once a St Sulien. However, I'll support Tyssul's theory.

Tyssul and Maggie are not on the telephone so we communicated at first by postcard; before my visit, Maggie wrote in her directions that I was to look out for a steel caravan. However, the first thing I saw when I drove up the track to the caravan site was a grazing zebra and a girl with a bowl walking towards a reclin-ing camel. They were part of a circus which had pulled in on a piece of land just over the hedge from the small cluster of living vans constituting the caravan site. Tyssul and Maggie's eye-catching, steel-bodied Westwood Ranger trailer was easy to spot amongst the other vans, and after our introductions I said how smart the trailer looked.

Tyssul replied: 'It's quite famous, it's been on TV. It was the one in which Seth of *Emmerdale Farm* was kidnapped, though that was before I had it. I saw it for sale at a garage and bought at the beginning of this year, just after our daughter Margaret died, to cheer us really.'

Tyssul then explained that their daughter Margaret, aged thirty, had died of cancer of the liver and pancreas. Understandably he and Maggie are deeply upset at her loss, but it has affected Tyssul in another way, too, in that it has rekindled his determination to fight for more permanent sites for travellers. This is because near the time of Margaret's death the family were living in a council house, as all the travellers' sites were full; but Margaret was used to travelling life, and expressed a wish to die in a caravan. A relative of Tyssul's mother had a field which he'd opened for travellers, and Tyssul wanted to take Margaret to it – but unfortunately the site had been closed because it wasn't legal, and so Tyssul couldn't get permission to take his caravan there. As a result, Margaret died in the house.

(opposite and above) Tyssul and Maggie Burton in front of their eye-catching, steel-bodied caravan

Tyssul is bitter: 'The Criminal Justice Act finished us. It doesn't compel councils to provide sites, but it gives power to authorities to move us on. We've had to shift four times in one day. All travellers are persecuted, even if they are on a site. If I had a passport I wouldn't be classed as a British citizen, they'd put "gypsy" on it.

'It's a worse thing when our kids go to school, they get taunted; and I remember that when I was working, say I'd strip down and mend an engine, other workers would say, "How do you learn that, gippo?" I'm going on sixty-one years old, and I've never owed money in my life.'

Despite their troubles Tyssul and Maggie were kindly and hospitable, and Tyssul was always ready to tell a story and joke over it with Maggie. They keep a canary, a goldfinch, and a canary crossed with a finch in separate cages in their trailer. Tyssul admitted that he loved birds, and I asked if he'd ever considered getting a parrot. Maggie exclaimed: 'Heaven forbid, he talks enough without a parrot, too!'

Tyssul retorted that he'd once owned some monkeys, or at least his mother had: 'Gypsies think monkeys unlucky, but a family named Black had two sons in the Merchant Navy and they once brought back two monkeys for Mother. They were called Tecko and Frank. We had 'em in the house and treated 'em like kids. Once when Gran, Mother's mother, came to stay, she got out all the stuff for making pancakes – you know, flour and so on – and then she left it a short while. When she came back the monkeys had tossed it everywhere, the house was milk-white with flour. We used to take them out in the lorry just like a dog. They could be bloody vicious. They died of pneumonia when they were about ten or twelve years old.'

Tyssul told me that he would have liked to have gone into the army, a family tradition, but he failed to get in. Nevertheless he has had interesting and varied work during his life: he has driven long-distance lorries; helped to build dams; spent twenty-two years in Aberystwyth 'doing work on tunnels'; and been a mechanic and prop charge-hand on feature films at Pinewood Studios. In between times he's done a bit of dealing, and this has included a few odd transactions; in his own words:

'I once swapped a horse to Bertram Mills for an American saddle of blue leather, but it weighed half a hundredweight and any horse would go bandy carrying it. So I sold it. Another time, when I was living in Aberystwyth, I advertised a Vauxhall car and some furniture for sale, and a boy from the college came and bought both and paid by cheque. The cheque was foreign, I didn't understand it, so I was at the bank at nine o'clock the next morning; they told me the boy was King Feizal's grandson, and his father could probably have bought the whole of Aberystwyth!'

(left) The young couple: Tyssul and Maggie
(opposite) Maggie's Grannie Boswell and
Maggie's parents

Tyssul and Maggie married when they were both twenty-four. Maggie told me that her mother was Abegail Ann Boswell, but she was generally known as Minnie; she was the daughter of Anna May Boswell. She has clear recollections of her childhood: 'Grannie owned a fair, that is swing-boats, a small roundabout, a hoopla, a small ride and rifles. They'd travel around Cardiganshire with it, and always kept the rides nicely painted up. When Mum married, Dad helped with the fair, too. In between times they did other work as they moved about. He was a scrap merchant; he'd collect scrap and pack it into our lorry and take it to the nearest dealer.

'Mum and I went out with our baskets, hawking. We'd sell pegs and bits of drapery and cups and saucers from the potteries in Staffordshire. They were seconds, and we got them sent to the nearest station. Sometimes we went with Dad, sometimes on foot. There was no set route, we'd stop a day or two in each place, and when trade went slack, move on. We had a living van pulled by two horses which we tethered in the lanes and on commons.

'Gypsy women then always wore black pinneys which we sent off for. They had big patch pockets and were plain, but you could sew whatever design you wanted onto the bodice which had twelve to fourteen buttons down the front.'

Tyssul and Maggie then reminisced about food cooked on an outdoor fire in a 'crock 'un' (an iron pot) suspended from a 'carvery kosh' (a kettle iron), and both insisted that 'food didn't taste half as good cooked on a stove'. Outdoor life was something to which Maggie had introduced Tyssul, because his own family had settled into a house when he was five years old. Tyssul explained: 'She encouraged me to move about, and when we married I bought a new Blue Bird Teenager caravan. I liked it because I was always bit of a roamer.'

I asked Tyssul to tell me about his background, and this is his story:

'My mother's maiden name was Edwards, and she came from North Wales. Her father worked in a slate quarry until there was a strike, and then the quarry owners took the roofs off the workers' houses and drove them out. Grandfather went with his brothers around the Aberystwyth area calling at farms repairing clocks. They'd leave a little mark in the back of each to remind them how much they'd charged, so they'd know if they came back the following year.

'When I was twelve or thirteen there was a meeting in Cory Hall, Cardiff, for everyone with the surname of Edwards. A wealthy man called Edwards had died in America and they were trying to find a William Edwards named in his will so that this man could claim what was called the "Edwards' millions". Grandfather went to the meeting because it had always been told in mother's family how her ancestors went out to America with the first settlers.

An informal portrait of the young couple on the step of their caravan

They'd bought land off the Indians and built a bridge, and later the Yankees had bought the mineral rights to their land, and they had a lot of money. My grandfather asked the *News of the World* to help him trace his ancestors back that far, and they did, but he couldn't prove he was a relative of the man that died and the money went unclaimed.

'There was another family story that one of mother's family called William Edwards was killed in the battle of Alamo in which Davey Crockett died, and Colonel William Travis. Then a few years ago a young friend of ours went to San Antonio in Texas, and when he came back told us he'd seen a grave there to "William Edwards, late of Aberystwyth, Wales". Oddly enough an old chap down here bought some silver spurs from a woman up north who said that they'd belonged to Colonel Travis; but he sold 'em.

'On the Burton side of the family, Father's parents came from Pencader; Grandfather bought a place there in 1911. He was a horse dealer – he used to buy horses for the army, and a vet would come from Melton Mowbray and pick the ones they wanted. Grandfather was the first bloke in Carmarthenshire to have a one-ton Ford "Tin Lizzie"; he bought it in 1911 for £110.

'Grandmother's maiden name was Morris. Her brother Ted Morris used to make buckets. He'd go to the Pontarddulais Plate Works and arrange for them to send tin to the nearest railway station, and he'd collect it with a horse and cart. Once when I was delivering to a farm in Brecon I saw some of his buckets – I knew they were my great-uncle's because of their shape, it was the way he made them.

'Father had six brothers, and one of them had a tame little fox which had been lamed by a trap. Once day at Pencader the boy and Grannie were out on their cart, and a local farmer came up and said, "Where's the fox?" – and Grannie said, "He's here, on my boy's lap"; and the farmer hit her and took her eye out. He was taken to court, but not a lot was done about it.'

Tyssul paused before giving the following aside: "Ham Bones" we call farmers; we don't like them. One time there was one in the dentist's waiting whilst I was having a tooth out. I won't have injections because they won't "take" on me. Maggie was in the waiting room. When the dentist was pulling the tooth blood spurted everywhere – I remember I said "Sorry about your white coat" to the dentist. While this was happening the door opened and the farmer in the waiting room was terrorised, he fainted straight out!

'I remember one of my uncles had terrible toothache one day when he was driving along in his lorry. He stopped at a house and asked the woman there to boil his pliers in a saucepan and she asked him why, and he said because he was going to use them to pull his tooth out – and he did.'

Tyssul resumed his narrative about his direct relatives: 'Father was a horse dealer, he bought and sold Welsh Cobs and Arabs. He used to do business with farmers, and at marts like the one at Llanbydder. He also used to sell piebald horses to circuses. I was born in a horse-drawn caravan at Clynderwen in 1936. I didn't have any brothers or sisters.

'During the war my parents were in Trecwn, near Fishguard; we were living in a large bus then. One day Father and his mate saw a bloke sat on a milk stand. He was wearing new boots and had a long ginger beard, and he was reading a map. He said to them, "How far to Aberporth, and what country roads can I follow to get there?" There was a rocket research range at Aberporth and so my father was suspicious. He said to the man, "When did you have food last? Come and have a cup of tea." It was the new boots made him suspicious, too, because at that time you never saw new boots. When they got home, Father told my mother in Romani to get the police – but the man jumped the door and ran off. Three days later he was found in a valley near Fishguard and was shot.

'Talking of the war,' Tyssul continued, 'in about 1960 me and the wife was in Brawdy, near St David's, buying scrap. We were at a farm, and while we were there a Volkswagen camper van pulled into the yard and the driver, a German, asked the farmer where the big well in the quarry was. He told the farmer that during the war he used to pull his submarine in nearby and siphon fresh water out of the well with some pipes. The spot was very close to a fighter base.

'When I was five, father bought a little field at Trecwn, built a house on it and sold the caravan. He also bought the grazing rights on twenty-five acres of common at Fishguard. Oddly enough he didn't like travellers, and the reason he bought the rights was to get them off it. We used to sell firewood and scrap, and father kept a lot of poultry. Every Christmas he'd sell forty geese, a hundred ducks and two hundred cockerels.

'Through living close to Fishguard I got to know it well. It's an Irish town really, with all the

Here is a gypsy superstition recounted by Tyssul:

'If a weasel crosses the road in front of you, that foretells coming bad luck.'

* * *

Weasels have long been associated with bad luck. Three old rhymes, the first two Scottish and the third Irish, mention this:

"A man mun ride when he canna wressel,
    But if at starting he sees a weasel
Gan weddershins around a stane,
    His hore'll sune be back its lane."

"Gin yer gan te meet yer lassie,
    An' a wesel chance te pass ye,
Ye'd better bide at hame that day,
    She'll be as soor as lapper's whey."

"If ye go fishin' or sweet-heartin',
    And meet a weasel when ye're starting',
It's divil a throut that day ye'll be killing',
    And ye'll find the the lady verry unwillin'."

Irish going to and fro on the ferry. I became fascinated by the Irish and by Ireland, and one day when I was a teenager I got onto the ferry and when it docked at Rosslare I walked and thumbed lifts the 110 miles to Dublin. I went to sleep on a park bench in Dublin, and one of the gardeners called the police. A policeman came and told me he was taking me back to "barracks", but at the police station he gave me breakfast. I told him my address at home. He rang a farmer who took me on to help get his harvest in. I was in Ireland three months.'

Tyssul finished telling of his father's side of the family with the following sad story:

'Grandfather Burton eventually went to live with his son, Bishop, in Cardigan. When he was ninety he was on his own in the house one day and he dropped his pipe, and it set the house alight and he was burnt to death.'

Maggie lifted a seat cover, and from the storage space beneath, pulled out a fat book. It had been published in America and was called something like *The Burton Book*. It contained the origin of the surname Burton, and thousands of names and addresses of Burtons; Tyssul said that theirs were in it somewhere. He also showed me another treasure, an old peg-knife he'd kept over the years. Meanwhile Maggie was making mugs of good, strong tea, and then she and Tyssul renewed their cigarettes.

Next, Tyssul told me more about his campaign for permanent sites for travellers, one which he'd started twelve or thirteen years previously, at first to help himself, then to fight for others, too. He now has the title 'Gypsy Spokesman' and, together with his friend 'Nick the Russian' (because he's of Russian birth), has even appeared on television programmes to speak up for gypsies. He is understandably sensitive to derision from gorgios, but deals with it in his own way, as he describes thus: 'There was a chap running down travellers who was no better than he ought to have been. I knew he'd stolen items from shops, something which I'd never do, and so I put the evil-eye on him, wished it on him: I said "You'll die, and no one will find you for days" – and that's what happened.'

I was a bit sceptical: 'Couldn't that have been coincidence? There isn't really such a thing as the evil-eye, is there?'

But Tyssul was adamant: 'There is. When I was a kid a travelling woman called Marjorie Lovell used to put "the eye" on people. Everyone was frightened of her and never insulted her; even the police inspector would pick her up and give her a lift if she was out walking. Once she wanted a loaf but knew she couldn't get to the shop before it closed, so stopped at a farm to ask for some bread. The farmer kicked her up the behind, but she told him, "In twelve months time you'll be dead, and I'll be passing your coffin on the road"; and she did.'

A poem composed by Tyssul and written down for him by a friend:

LUCY

Lucy is a pretty girl
So Young and unaware;
She thinks that Gorgio
Is Equal, Just and fair

A Dream that when she's older
She'll travel like her mum;
Flow on night-time's river
Sail on roads beneath the sun

I worry for the day
That Lucy sees the suss,
That life just isn't easy
Living in a bus.

Why, that when she's older,
Her lifestyle will be banned;
And it will be a crime
to move across the land.

Oh, Lucy, I pity you
Your future isn't good;
They'll always want to hound you,
They won't leave you like they should.

But still, you're just a little child
And these problems aren't yet real,
So stay in your perfect world
With the freedom you do feel.

Talking about the evil-eye led to our discussing gypsy superstitions generally; according to Tyssul: 'A weasel crossing the road in front of you is unlucky – whenever it happened to me I've had bad luck. Once I was done by the police straight afterwards for a bad handbrake, and another time I went a short way and became involved in an accident.'

And Maggie said: 'Crows are unlucky. If my brother sees a single one in a field he'll go home. There are also certain flowers you don't bring indoors, like snowdrops and mayflower. Bluebells are unlucky too, they droop which is a sign of death.' However, mention of flowers prompted Tyssul to recall the good properties some have: 'I was born blind. About a year later we were pulled in on a farm and the local shepherd brought a big bunch of eyebright down from the hills and told my mother to stew it and use the water to bathe my eyes. She did, and they got better.'

I asked Tyssul if he knew any old gypsy cures, and he said that he'd learnt some for horses from his father. 'For bots he used the leaves of a box tree, dried them in the oven like sage and then powdered them into linseed oil. That makes horses pass bots. And when a horse got grass disease he used to make up a spoonful of linseed oil and turps for it.'

'What's grass disease?'

'They swell up and their nostrils get large and they die. Another thing my father once did, he bought a horse as old as the hills from a farmer and had to walk it twenty miles to get it back home; it almost finished the horse. Then he went to the local ironmonger's and bought some 12-bore cartridges and a pint of linseed oil. He put the black powder from the cartridges into the linseed oil and gave it to the horse up its nostrils. In the field the horse was full of life. Father sold it to an old trapper called Monty who'd been attacked by a donkey when he was a young man and it had eaten his arm and leg. Monty wanted something cheap, and Father said he could have the horse for £15; he'd paid £12 10s for it himself. He said, "You keep dredging and he'll be OK." That 'orse lived for about eight or nine months.'

Tyssul added that he could effect cures, too. 'A gentleman down the road had a colt run into barbed wire. I'd bought a transit van off him and left the spare wheel there, and this happened when I was picking the wheel up. The colt cut his chest so badly he'd have been scarred for life, but I went into the chemist's in Kidwelly, bought some chemicals, I won't say what they were, washed the wound with warm water and salt and rubbed the chemicals in. It healed the horse.

'In fact I used the same mixture in Carmarthen market the other day. There's a lady there with a stall where I buy a few bits and pieces, and she was worried about her dog losing its fur; so I gave her the mixture and said, "That'll bring the fur back."' At this he grinned, and running his fingers through his auburn hair said ruefully: 'It doesn't work on humans, though.' His hair, however, looked rather like his fund of stories – plentiful enough without encouragement.

Before I left, Tyssul and Maggie said that if I knew of anyone who'd help them with their campaign against the Criminal Justice Act and plead their cause for a permanent travellers' site at Carmarthen, they'd be grateful to hear. 'The morning cry rang out – there's no surrender!' Tyssul called over the caravan door at my departing back. 'That's from the Civil War in Spain in 1936 – I had family out there – a lot of Welsh went out to fight.'

TALES OF GYPSY KINGS & QUEENS

THE FAAS

In 1540 James V of Scotland gave John Faa a writ which confirmed Faa's authority over rebellious members of his tribe. Faa was described as 'lord and earl of Little Egypt'. One of his predecessors, Sir John Faa, is commemorated in a more popular way in the ballad *The Gypsy Laddie*. The story goes that in 1643, he ran off with Jean, Countess of Casillis of Casillis Castle, Ayrshire, whilst her husband was away; in fact Sir John had been her lover before her marriage. When the earl returned he set off in pursuit of the kidnapping band, and took his revenge by killing fifteen of them at a place on the River Doon, subsequently known as the 'Gypsies' Steps'. The ballad tells of Jean's willing abduction:

> *The Gypsies cam' to my lord's yett,*
> *And O but they sang sweetly;*
> *They sang sae sweet, and sae very compleat,*
> *That doun cam' our fair ladye.*
>
> *And she cam' tripping doun he stair,*
> *And all her maids before her:*
> *As sune as they saw her weel-faured face,*
> *They cuist the glamourye owre her.*
>
> *'O come wi' me', says Johnny Faa,*
> *'O come wi' me, my dearie;*
> *For I vow and swear, by the hilt of my sword,*
> *That your Lord sall nae mair come near ye.'*

The Faas moved from Scotland to England at the beginning of the eighteenth century. Will Faa (mentioned by Sir Walter Scott) ruled as King of the Gypsies in the south, and was succeeded by his eldest son William. The family had settled by this time at Yetholm in the border country. When William died he was succeeded by his sister's son Charles Blythe who was married to Esther Faa (thought to be a cousin). Their son David, born in

1795, declined to assume the title of 'King' on his father's death, and instead David's sister became 'Queen Esther'.

Although he renounced his regal title, David Blythe was enough of a character to have a book written about him when he died in 1883. Its author, Charles Stuart, was a doctor and keen naturalist. He writes of David Blythe's knowledge of the flora and fauna of the borders, but every now and again he includes an anecdote which brings out the gypsy's character. For example, this is Blythe's own tale:

David Blythe, aged 82

About fifty years ago I was at Greenlaw Fir, busy unpacking my dishes before placing them on ma stand, when Mr. D _____ o' F_____ cleugh, booted and spurred, at the tail o' a wheen shairny beasts, comes richt through the middle o' mu crockery, breaking ever so many jugs and basins. Says I, 'Mr. D_____, you'll hae to pay me for this damage done'. 'Awa wi' you and your mugs, I hae nae time the day to be bathered wi' ye,' replies the farmer. So aff I goes to the Rev. A. Home, the minister o' the parish, and Justice o' the Peace, and asks him what I am to dae. The minister declined to interfere. Man, I never could bide priests ever since. Comin' alang the road I meets Mr. Bell, the town clerk o' Dunse, and details ma case. 'Just you go to my clerk at the Town Hall, give him sixpence, and he'll tell you what to do.' 'Summon him to Dunse Court, of course,' says the clerk; and Mr. D _____ was summoned at once. It was a fine warm summer day the court day, and ma cairt was lowsed in the Market Square at Dunse, and I was lying on some street atween the trams, when by comes Mr. D ____. Says he, 'It's a fine warm day. Come awa up to 'The Horn', and I'll give ye a bottle o' yill, and settle this business.' 'Na, na!' says I, 'it's owre warm the day.' So at the court the Sheriff asks Mr. D _____ the reason why he did not repay me for the damage, and said he wondered how he allowed such a case to come before a court, ordering the amount claimed to be paid at once. Meeting Mr. D _____ leaving the court, I said till him 'I wonder a gentleman like you would come to Dunse on the summons o' a mugger!

THE NORWOOD GYPSIES

During the seventeenth and eighteenth centuries, gypsy encampments by woodland in Norwood on the outskirts of London were well known. When the poet Byron was a schoolboy in Norwood he visited them, and rich and poor came from the city to hear the gypsies tell their fortunes; even the Prince of Wales (George III) visited.

The most famous of the Norwood gypsies is Margaret Finch, known as Queen Margaret.

Margaret Finch, Queen of the Gypsies at Norwood

She died in 1740 aged 109. Because she had spent so long sitting with her knees drawn up under her chin, and probably also due to arthritis, her joints had locked, so that when she died her limbs couldn't be straightened out; because of this she was buried in a square coffin, at Beckenham Parish Church. Local publicans paid for her funeral as a token of their gratitude for the custom her fortune-telling had brought them!

Margaret's niece Bridget succeeded to the title of Queen of the Gypsies. She died in 1768 and is buried at Dulwich. The next recorded queen (in 1790) was a grand-daughter of Margaret and a niece of Bridget. This queen lived next door to a public house called 'The Gypsy House.'

The Norwood gypsy encampments were finally broken up by raids from the police, and the land was eventually developed, the villa-type houses which became popular in the early nineteenth century being built on it. Those gypsies who wanted to stay in the area – and many did – had to become house-dwellers and settle into the gorgio community.

Norwood's connection with gypsies is perpetuated by local names. There is Gypsy Hill, Gypsy Road, Romany Road and Finch Avenue. There is also The Gypsy Queen pub in Norwood High Street, and The Gypsy Hill Tavern on, of course, Gypsy Hill. Moreover there is no indication that these pubs will follow the fashion of having their names altered to a more whimsical appellation, for The Gypsy Tavern has recently had its sign of a caravan, gypsy and crystal ball handsomely repainted.

ISAAC HERNE

When Isaac Herne died aged ninety at Sutton-on-Trent during the night of 21–22 February 1911, gypsies and gypsiologists mourned his passing. Looked up to as their Sherengro (chief) he was from one of the oldest known Romani families. There was not a single drop of giorgio blood in his veins, and one newspaper went so far as to print: 'He had a pedigree and an escutcheon as long and as undefiled as might have excited the envy and admiration of many an English aristocrat.' Isaac himself had used a more straightforward way of describing old Romani bloodstock, stating simply that they were 'the real standard people, the truth of England'.

Isaac's father was Nearbi Herne and his mother Sinfai, 'the Crow'; she was said to have taught George Borrow 'deep' (the purest form of) Romani. During his lifetime Isaac occasionally talked of Borrow, whom he remembered; he described him as: 'Almost a giant – a very noble-looking gentleman, as it might be Mayor of England.'

Isaac's cousin Sanspirella married Jasper Petulengro, immortalised in Borrow's *Lavengro* and *Romany Rye*. Isaac himself married Sinfai, the daughter of Piramus Grey, who was mentioned in *Romany Rye* as being a good shot, an excellent fiddler and a dour fighter. Sinfai died in 1906, and according to custom Isaac burnt her caravan and all her belongings. At his own death the following arrangements are reported to have taken place:

An oak coffin large enough to contain his body, and clothes and most cherished possessions – his pipe, and watch, and knife etc – was ordered from the village carpenter. As soon as the body had been enclosed in it, his favourite horse was harnessed to his van, containing all his remaining personal property, and led into an adjoining field. There the unoffending animal was shot, and, after lights had been applied to the inflammable contents of the van, its body was added to the funeral pyre thus raised. As soon as this had spent itself the band of mourners took the ashes and sprinkled them all over the field; all of which was done by the last request of the dead man, and according to the ancient Romani custom. Ever since the 'Annual Register' in 1773 recorded the burning of Queen Diana Boswell's clothes in the Mint, Southwark, there has been a continual stream of testimony to the performance of this rite, especially in England. Probably it has its roots in the fear of the Gypsies lest the spirits of the dead should return to haunt those things which had been so closely associated with them on earth, for all good Gypsies believe in, and are thoroughly afraid of spirits. But possibly it may have arisen from a loving desire to provide for their transference to the other world, and their material comfort there. In connection with this latter theory I am tempted to mention a story told of a Gypsy who tossed down a half-crown into a dead friend's open grave, remarking solemnly as he did so, 'Here, Jimmy, my lad, here's something to wet your whistle on the way'. It goes without saying that the custom is wasteful in the extreme. The value of the articles destroyed by the Hernes amounted to £70. Luckily they are a wealthy family, but had they been compelled to choose between poverty and the non-observance of the sacrificial rite, they would unhesitatingly have chosen poverty.

Isaac's wish was that he be buried beneath the shade of a hedge in Manston Churchyard, Leeds. The rector of Manston, Mr Herbert Malleson had been his friend and was a gypsiologist. The above description of Isaac's funeral comes from papers kept by Mr Malleson.

XAVIER PETULENGRO

Xavier is better known as 'Gypsy Petulengro'; his mother, a Romanian gypsy, prophesied on her death-bed that he would speak to millions who would never see his face. She died when the wireless was still in its experimental stages and had never heard of it, but in March 1934 her son gave a talk on BBC radio about Romany remedies and recipes, and it was so popular that he was asked to give others. Interest in his talks increased during the war years, because his Romany tips on collecting and cooking from the wild dovetailed with the Ministry of Food's own campaign to promote 'hedgerow harvests' of berries, nuts and plants to boost meagre food rations.

Gypsy Petulengro's grandfather Ambrose Smith had been George Borrow's Tinker Jasper Petulengro. His father was a trader in Welsh ponies who travelled overseas, and in so doing had met and married his wife Anyeta. The family came back to live in England when Xavier was a small boy.

Petulengro had an extraordinary life. He learned horse-trading from his father, but to escape the legal consequences of a fight with a gamekeeper he joined the army. In fact he served twice in the army, the second time as a cavalryman. Coming back to his family he hawked hand-made goods, and collected herbs which he sold to chemists. He went to America several times, at one point there calling himself Dr Thompson, 'Son of professor Theodore Sylvanus Thompson, the celebrated British scientist'. As Dr Thompson he sold, very successfully, pills he made from a 'special' herb; he also travelled with a fair in America; and he spent some time as the manager of a workforce on a plantation. He was imprisoned in Brazil, and prospected for diamonds in South Africa. In England he had a stint as a violinist in a major orchestra; and in his later years he sold his wares in a depart-

Viney Hill Church

184

ment store – this was because the takings were good, although he hated the surroundings.

Petulengro never married. When he was a young man the girl he'd loved was kicked by a horse and died of her injuries. In their courting days she had laughingly taken his hand and told him, 'You will hold more racklers' duks in your duk than any man in England.' In his fascinating autobiography *A Romany Life* he confirms the truth of those words, stating: 'I have held more women's hands in mine than any man living, as many as two hundred a day passing through my hands to be read.'

In 1929 the town of Baildon on the Yorkshire moors revived its Gipsy Party, an event which generations earlier had been started by genuine gypsies; for the 1929 revival, however, most of the revellers were townspeople dressed up as gypsies. The 'Party' was a success, and others followed. For the 1937 one, the organisers invited Gypsy Petulengro, and he was crowned 'King of the Gypsies' at a spectacular ceremony.

A young gypsy couple, Leon Petulengro and Eileana Smith, were married at the local church on the same day, and directly afterwards 'King' Petulengro conducted a second ceremony which married them according to Romani rites. The event involved blood-mingling and jumping over a fire, and was much photographed – newsreel companies even sent film crews to cover it.

The 1937 ceremony confirmed Petulengro's place amongst the popular press as 'King of Britain's Romanies' for the remaining twenty years of his life. He lived to be ninety-eight, and died at Littlehampton in Sussex. In his lifetime Gypsy Petulengro had been friends with a Mr and Mrs George Vines who lived at Church View, Viney Hill in the Forest of Dean; in fact he had visited them only eighteen months before his death. He had requested that he be buried at Viney Hill Church across the way from the Vines' house. The funeral service was organised by his sister Lavanya, and a gypsy band of three violins and a piano accordion preceded his coffin to the grave, which is situated near the west wall of the church.

PRESENT DAY

Gypsies today say that there are no such persons as gypsy kings and queens, and that these are only media terms. However, they admit that certain of their number are held in great respect, and Billie Welch of Darlington is one. He holds the post of Sherro Rom (head man) at Appleby Fair. He is a slightly built, elegantly turned-out man with a pencil-thin moustache, and he wears an antique Freemason's ring. He is literate, well-to-do and altogether venerable, and has the ability to speak eloquently on behalf of gypsies.

I managed to talk briefly to him. He told me that he is a 'Sinti Romani', and that Sinti is one of the four true Romani tribes. It is obvious from the following tale he related that he is from proud stock: 'One day my grandfather, together with other gypsies, had been invited onto Lord Lonsdale's estate to course their dogs. Lord Lonsdale used to watch, and he'd buy the best dogs. Grandfather was holding his dog by his silk scarf, but unfortunately the scarf slipped and the dog started too soon. "Very unsporting!" Lord Lonsdale said. But Grandfather said quickly, "I'll take that off no man. Not even you. I might be lame, but I can stand up for myself!" And he made to fight Lord Lonsdale. Fortunately he was stopped by the other men present.'

Billie said that his father had been one of the largest horse dealers in the country. It is hardly surprising that Billie himself is looked up to in the gypsy community, for he has done several 'good works' on their behalf. For example, about twenty years ago he provided

Lord Lonsdale

a much-needed caravan site for them in Darlington. One mark of the respect in which he's held is that his presence is valued at funerals. He admitted wryly that he seems to go to more funerals than a funeral director, and if he is unable to attend, then one of his four sons represents him. He explained that gypsy funerals can be massive affairs, with the coffin left open for a week beforehand so that people can stay in the vicinity and show their respects. Marriages also make for large gatherings because families are so big. When one of his sons was married not long ago, he hired Walworth Castle for the reception and had an open bar for between five hundred and six hundred people!

Speaking of marriage, Billie – who incidentally is known as Uncle Billie, 'Uncle' being a gypsy term of respect – said that gypsies have a high moral code, and that there are very few divorces. He added: 'In my grandfather's time, if you married out [to a non-gypsy] you were left out. You were also left out for child molestation, rape and violence – banished forever, out in the wilderness.'

Not long after we spoke, Billie went into hospital for quite a long spell; when he came out he had to deal with a backlog of his business affairs, so we never met up again. However, I was to encounter his name once more. This came about because he had told me that one of the Darlington cemeteries was renowned for its gypsy memorial stones, so one day I went to look at them. In the cemetery was a young woman tending a child's grave; her name was Pamela, and the grave was that of her five-year-old son Sean, tragically killed in a road accident. Aged twenty-five, she had never organised a funeral, and the task of doing it for her own son had completely overwhelmed her. She was a gorgio, but her friends were gypsies and they had helped her, even arranging with the police to have the route the cortège would take, coned off and policed. Her friends on Billie Welch's caravan site had clubbed together and paid for flowers for Sean. There were many beautiful ones on his grave, some making up the traditional gypsy memorials of 'Heaven's Gate' and the 'Empty Chair'. 'The vacant chair is in heaven for him,' Pamela explained. She added gratefully: 'There's sufficient money left from what they gave to buy a headstone too, in time.'

ACKNOWLEDGEMENTS

I am indebted to each interviewee for contributing reminiscences and photographs and for their kindness to me in my endeavours to compile this book. Thank you.

I would also like to acknowledge and thank the following for their invaluable help in supplying information and reference and archive material:

Bradford Central Library; The Craven Museum, Skipton; The Crown Inn, Woolhope, Herefordshire; Croydon Local Studies Library; Gloucester Records Office; Hereford County Records Office; Hampshire County Council's Gypsy Liaison Officer, George Summers; the Staff of Ledbury Library; The University of Liverpool Special Collections and Archives Department; The Norwood Society; Portsmouth City Council Library Service (Historical Collections); the Romany and Traveller Family History Society; the late Roy Sewell; Shropshire Records Office; The Earl of Selborne KBE, FRS; John Smith, Archives Officer, Church Army Headquarters; Lady Juliet Townsend; Worcestershire County Museum.

I am grateful for the guidance of my editor Sue Viccars and her editorial colleagues. Indeed, I thank all at my publishers who have helped this book on its way.

* * *

The author and publishers would like to thank the following people for supplying photographs for this book:

Mr & Mrs T. Burton pp174, 175(both), 176; Church Army Archives pp14–15, 142, 148, 149, 150, 151; Mr & Mrs T. Coulson pp122, 123, 124(btm), 125, 126(both), 127(both), 128(btm); Mr & Mrs W. Coulson p118(both); Crown Inn, Woolhope, Herefordshire p12; Croydon Local Studies Library p182; Mr & Mrs E. Frankham pp24, 26, 27(top), 28, 29, 32, 34; Harriet Hall p38; Bill Harrison pp163(all), 164(top & btm), 166(top); Dick Harrison pp162(btm), 165, 171(top); Mr & Mrs Jim Harrison p169(btm); Mr & Mrs K. Hawkins pp131, 132, 133, 134(both); Hereford County Records Office pp70, 91; Jean Hudson pp4, 168(btm), 169(top), 170(btm), 171(btm); Peter Ingram pp82, 103; University of Liverpool Special Collections and Archives Department pp3, 8, 10, 16, 73, 78, 90, 92, 93, 96, 105; Portsmouth City Council Library Service (Historical Collection) p27(btm); Len Smith (via Church Army Archives) pp135, 144; Sotheby's p2; Lady Juliet Townsend pp97, 98.

All other photographs are by the author.

The illustrations on pp44, 49 and 52 originally appeared in *Dene Forest Sketches*; those on pp30 and 144(top) appeared in *Among the Hop Pickers*; the illustration on p181 appeared in *David Blyth – The Gypsy King*. (Details of all titles are given in the Bibliography.)

BIBLIOGRAPHY

Birkenhead, Lord *Lady Eleanor Smith – A memoir* (Hutchinson, 1953)

Bowness, Charles *Romany Magic* (The Aquarian Press, 1974 edition)

Chinn, Samuel *Among the Hop Pickers* (John F. Shaw & Co, 1887)

Clinch, George *English Hops: A History of Cultivation and Preparation for the Market from Earliest Times* (McCorquodale & Co Ltd, 1919)

Coulter, John *Norwood Past* (Historical Publications Ltd, 1996)

Crawley Boevey, S.M. *Dene Forest Sketches* (John and Robert Maxwell, *c*1900)

Galer, Allan M. *Norwood Past & Present* (Local History Reprints, 1995)

Gipsy Petulengro, *A Romany Life* (Methuen & Co, 1935)

Leland, C.E. *Gypsy Sorcery & Fortune Telling* (London, 1891)

Lynch, Donald *Chariots of the Gospel* (Eyre & Spottiswoode, 1982)

Okely, Judith *Changing Cultures: The Traveller Gypsies* (Cambridge University Press, 1983)

Rowan, Edgar *Wilson Carlile & The Church Army* (Hodder & Stoughton, 1906)

Smith, Eleanor *Life's A Circus* (Longmans, Green & Co, 1939)

Smith, Hubert *Tent Life with English Gypsies in Norway* (1873)

Stuart, Charles MD EDIN *David Blythe – The Gypsy King* (J. & J.H. Rutherford, Kelso, 1883)

Wagner, Sir Anthony *English Geneology* (Phillimore, 1983)

Ward Jackson, C.H. & Harvey, Denis E. *The English Gypsy Caravan* (David & Charles, 1989 edition)

Warwick, Alan *The Phoenix Suburb* (Norwood Society, 1991)

White, Gilbert *The Natural History and Antiquities of Selborne in the County of Southampton* (Macmillan & Co Ltd, 1905)

Yates, Dora E. *My Gypsy Days – Recollections of a Romani Rawnie* (Phoenix House Ltd, 1953)

NEWSPAPERS & PERIODICALS

Bradford Telegraph & Argus (28 August 1937)

The Church Army Review (various dates)

Country Life (31 December 1953)

Daily Chronicle (20 February 1914)

Gloucester Citizen (17 June and 20 June 1957)

Illustrated Chronicle (11 March 1915)

Morning Leader (14 June 1907)

Romany Routes Vol 3 No 4

Pinks' Pictorial (July 1908)

Shropshire Magazine (December 1963)

The Yorkshire Observer Budget (4 September 1937)

INDEX